WHICH *fork* DO I USE?

WHICH *fork* DO I USE?

confident and comfortable dining

ROSEMARIE BURNS AND LINDA REED

TRAINED AND CERTIFIED BY
THE PROTOCOL SCHOOL OF WASHINGTON, WASHINGTON D.C.

Published by
Manners Simply

©2014 Rosemarie Burns and Linda Reed
Manners Simply
Danville, CA
orders@mannerssimply.com
www.mannerssimply.com

Manners Simply
P. O. Box 2676
Danville, California 94526

Design: Kathy Lee Williams, Lee Graphics, Los Gatos, CA
Typefaces: Adobe Garamond condensed for body, Futura medium condensed for subheads, Hanshand for titles
Printed in the USA

ISBN: 978-0-615-88318-2

First Edition
Which Fork Do I Use?
Confident and Comfortable Dining

10 9 8 7 6 5 4 3 2 1

Dedication

In loving memory of my sister, Mary Ann Pinguelo; my mother-in-law, Bingta Burns; and my aunt, Gladys Blankenship. Lastly, I dedicate this book to my resilient mother, Stella Baptista, who is 95 years old and counting.

I am truly blessed by the many ways each of you extraordinary women have touched my life and given me endless guidance and encouragement. Thank you for imprinting perseverance, kindness, eloquence and the meaning of family so deeply into my life. You will never be forgotten.

Acknowledgments

Stella Baptista, my mother, who's taught me that giving is far more important than receiving.

Jack Burns, my only child, whose support, wit, kindness and radiant attitude enriches the lives of all who know him, especially mine.

Kristina Burns, my daughter-in-law, who has put her heart and soul into raising my wonderful grandchildren. An avid cook and hostess herself, she and I have always shared recipes and a passion for cooking, dining and entertaining.

Jordan Burns, my grandson, who has great insights and can always calm me down with his carefree demeanor and the twinkle in his eye. He makes me very proud and brings me immense joy.

Gianna Burns, my granddaughter, so full of energy it's scary; she makes me laugh until I cry and her heart is as big as the sun. My life wouldn't be the same without you.

Julie Abuan and Dolores Serna, my sisters, who have taught me the meaning of always being there for each other. I am blessed to have such a close bond with you. Your love for me is unconditional, as mine is for you.

My lovely nieces and nephews, all of whom I cherish. Thank you for all the support, encouragement and love you have given me.

Connie McWhinney, my fashion forward step-daughter, who has a flair for bringing the family together and loves to dine and entertain with panache. Your generosity does not go unnoticed. I am so very thankful for having you in my life.

Sloane Pedersen, my selfless step-daughter, who has a heart of gold and relishes hosting guests in her new home. She stretches herself beyond words to please others. I am so very thankful for having you in my life.

Emerson and Calder McWhinney; Kathleen, Simeon and Farys Hixon, my sensationally creative step-grandchildren, whom I cherish and enjoy immensely.

Don Kingsborough, my mentor, confidant, staunch supporter, childhood friend and the brother I never had – irreplaceable!

Rebecca Kingsborough, we met over a pot of spilled beans; you are my best-of-the-best friends through happy and sad times. We are family in the purest sense. You are a precious gift from God.

To my golden best friends, Sandy Molinari, Pam Lindsey, Debra Miglia, Deanna Swanstrom, Kathy Burke, Genevieve Anderson, Lucille Santi, Margaret De Generro, Betty Couzens, Judy Maderious; along with my zealous foodie friends, the Dazzling Dazzlers – thank you for your stalwart, unwavering friendship.

Linda Reed. It was by chance that we met, but by choice that we became friends and business partners. We have finished our beloved book that we both are so proud of. Thank you for your hard work, patience, and tried-and-true friendship.

Allen Pedersen, whose abiding love amazes me daily. Thank you for all that you do and all that you are. After twenty-five years, "Yes, I will happily marry you!"

I am immensely grateful for each and every one of you and the relationships we have built. I value the genuine camaraderie we share and you are loved beyond measure. Without your influence, I would not have had the life experiences to co-create *"Which Fork Do I Use?"* In simple words, thank you.

~ *Rosemarie Burns*

Dedication

In memory of my salt-of-the-earth parents, Vonnie and Edith Harvey, who considered anyone who sat at our table family, and to my business partner and sister-in-life, Rosemarie Burns.

Acknowledgments

Edith Harvey, my mother, and Cora Daley, my grandmother, whose love and actions towards family continue to inspire me each day.

Lois Reed, my former mother-in-law, who first taught me to set the table correctly.

Irene Nelson, granny to many, who taught me the power of a lovingly baked cinnamon roll and how it bonds a family.

Lois Harvey, my sister-in-law, who showed me how to cook for the masses.

Gib Gettman, Jerry and Jack Sobotta, my early bosses at Hermiston Drug, where I fell in love with hand-cut crystal.

Ray and Clark Miller, the bosses who became family.

Barbara Palmer, my adopted mother-in-law, who has entrusted me with her family sterling silver.

Carlene Belisle (aka Mom Jr.) for your love, friendship and many hours of tirelessly serving as my assistant when I first started teaching etiquette classes.

Rosemary Baldo, Sondra Jameson, Lisa Baer, Jim and Linda France, Ron and Barbara Faunce – my steadfastly supportive friends! Jerry Singer and the Bubbleheads – for my continued education into the world of great champagne and food adventures.

Allen Pedersen, for all those trips to the airport and for being a great sounding board.

Tracey Cox, my beautiful niece, and her three daughters, Lily, Aubrey and Hadley; Jamie Baker, my beautiful niece, and her daughter, Aria; and my equally lovely step-daughter, Jaci Knittel, and her children, Mackenzie, Giselle and Jackson. You make my world a better place. I love you all beyond words.

Without the influence of each and every one of you, I would not have had the life experiences to co-create *"Which Fork Do I Use?"* In simple words, thank you.

~ *Linda Reed*

Introduction: Entertaining is Our Passion

Dining etiquette, manners and setting the table are becoming a lost art. Evidence of that is all around us. Busy lives keep families from sharing meals together. And we've all seen the couple at a restaurant or had guests in our homes, totally engaged with their mobile devices – "liking" their social media friends while ignoring those sitting right next to them.

The art of dining etiquette, manners and setting the table is based on skills which can be learned. Linda and I are proof of that. We sincerely believe that it's as important now as ever to know the basic rules of dining etiquette. Many life events, both social and business related, occur around dining together. It's in these situations that we are often judged by our behavior while dining. Landing that ideal job or getting promoted can depend on your ability to handle yourself well at the table. Making basic mistakes as a host or guest can be embarrassing, or result in others feeling uncomfortable. The reality is, opinions of us are formed by the way in which we dine.

Many of our students have assumed that since Linda and I teach etiquette we came from privileged backgrounds. Quite the contrary; our beginnings were humble. I grew up in a working class neighborhood in Oakland, California, while Linda grew up in a rural farming community in Oregon. We had rich but simple lives centered around family, food and friends.

We didn't know about table settings and certainly didn't know a thing about dining etiquette. Both Linda and I incorrectly learned to set the table with the knife, fork and spoon all to the right side of the plate. A normal night in my home was dinner served on an oilcloth tablecloth, or no tablecloth at all. Napkins weren't used in Linda's home, which may have been preferable to my house where we shared a communal dish towel. When I recently asked my 95-year-old mother, Stella, about the dish towel, she laughingly told me, "Well Honey, it had four corners to use. You girls each had a corner, and Dad and I had the middle."

Even though our mothers did their best to teach us table basics, it wasn't until our teenage years when we dined at the homes of friends and other family members that we discovered the table fundamentals experienced at home weren't always correct. It was then we began to recognize there was an entire world of knowledge and dining experiences we had not seen before.

Fortunately we had the pleasure of meeting wonderful and informed people who took us under their wings. Through them we learned the pleasure that comes from serving a delicious meal on a beautifully set table. They knew the rules, and we were inspired to learn them as well.

I chuckle when I look back at the times I ate my salad with the dessert fork. It was properly placed above the plate, but I didn't know which fork to use. For years Linda thought her beautiful sherry glasses were for white wine. Her friends must have thought she was a bit frugal for using such small glasses for their dinner wine. We didn't know what we didn't know, but it never stopped us from hosting dinner parties. The dinner parties graduated from simple barbecues to black tie events. The parties became more elaborate and more fun! Even with our vast dining experiences and knowledge, we have made mistakes along the way.

A desire for perfection drove Linda and me to seek more knowledge, confidence and refinement. We recognized the only way to achieve this personal growth was through expert training. It was this training that brought the two of us together at The Protocol School of Washington in our nation's capital. We mastered the coursework and have been teaching seminars together ever since. We are certified to instruct in the areas of American and Continental Styles of Dining, Social Etiquette, Tea and Etiquette, Business - International Etiquette and Protocol, and Dining and Etiquette for Children, Teens and Adults. We have a combined 43 years of experience in dining and etiquette seminar instruction. Our clients include Fortune 500 executives, business owners, college athletes, members of fraternal and professional organizations, international clients, aspiring young entrepreneurs, medical professionals, stay-at-home moms and dads, teens and children.

Linda and I share a passion for entertaining – we enjoy the entire experience. We absolutely love creating beautiful tables, designing menus and preparing meals. We recognize that deciding whom to invite to the party is every bit as important as a great meal. We feel that deciding on the right mix of guests is an art that is critical to an interesting evening full of great conversation and laughter.

A dinner party is a gift to family and friends. This gift is both simple and profound. A well-planned dinner party offers a good time and respite from the stresses of everyday life for guests.

Our goal is for hosts at any level of experience to be encouraged, inspired and confident enough to entertain and entertain well.

It brings us great joy and pride to have transformed our extensive experience in entertaining, dining and etiquette instruction into ***Which Fork Do I Use?***

~ *Rosemarie Burns*

Table of Contents

Basics of Setting the Table

"In order to break the rules of etiquette… you have to know what they are in the first place."

~ Letitia Baldrige

A well-dressed table enhances the dining experience. Setting the table is like getting dressed. You select an outfit which suits the occasion. In the same way, you choose a place setting which is appropriate to your menu. Tasteful accessories compliment your attire and express your individuality; likewise, linens and your centerpiece enhance the table's appearance. Your desired result – a stunning look that sets the dining mood.

TABLE TERMS and PROPER PLACEMENT

Table Pad - foldable, thick, felt-backed, vinyl-covered pads which are usually custom made.

Silence Cloth - thin cloth of flannel or felt-lined vinyl cut to the shape of your table. An inexpensive alternative to table pads.

Place your table pad or a silence cloth between the table and the tablecloth to add a softening barrier and to protect the tabletop from heat, spills and scratches.

Tablecloth - may be made from quality linen fabric, silk, cotton or vinyl. It protects the table from scratches, adds color and sets the tone of a meal or dinner party.

Tablecloths cover the tabletop and drape over the edge which is commonly called the drop. Drop lengths recommendations are a minimum 12 inches and no more than 18 inches. Buffet tables may have an 18-inch drop or floor length drop to cover unattractive table legs.

Napkin - may be cloth or paper and are part of each place setting. Diners use napkins to blot their lips and fingers throughout the meal.

Place napkins on the *left side* of the forks (if folded, the crease faces the plate), *under* the dinner plate or on *top* of the dinner plate. You may place the napkin under the forks on the left side of the place setting if you are restricted by space or setting the table outside where the wind might blow the napkins away. It is confusing to diners as to whose napkin is whose if you place napkins in a drink glass.

Napkin sizes: Dinner 20-26 inches, Luncheon 14-16 inches, Cocktail 5-7 inches.

Place Setting - also known as a cover, individual diner's section of the table which contains drink glasses, flatware, plates and napkin.

Align the place setting so that the middle of the dinner plate or charger is centered to the middle of each chair, *set one inch away from the table edge.* Allow a comfortable amount of space for each place setting; 24 inches from the center of one plate to another is adequate.

Place setting items (dinnerware, glassware, and flatware) may be all one pattern or mix-and-match.

Place Plate - an expensive china plate or a collector plate which is displayed as a piece of art, to be admired only.

It temporarily rests on the table for viewing as the guests arrive and are seated. Remove before any food service and replace with the first course plate.

Flora Danica
by Royal Copenhagen

Placemat - small mat beneath a place setting used to protect the table from food stains and spills. It may be decorative as well as functional and coordinated with napkins and other table decor.

Set the placemat one-half inch away from the edge of the table. A placemat remains on the table throughout the entire meal.

Charger - sometimes called a service plate, is an over-sized dinner plate which adds a touch of elegance and protection to the table top or linens. It eliminates the blank spot in front of the diner, and is placed slightly above the table edge at each place setting. All food-bearing dishes are placed on top of the charger. It is a matter of personal preference when the charger is removed, but it *must be removed prior to the dessert course.*

No food is served directly on a charger.

Choose your menu first

> The menu determines what dinnerware, glassware, and flatware you set at each place setting. If, for example, you are not serving champagne at your brunch, eliminate setting the champagne flute.

Dinnerware - also known as tableware, consists of plates and bowls for individual dining. Dinnerware can be made of the finest quality bone china, fine china, porcelain, stoneware, or earthenware. Plastic or paper is acceptable for casual use.

Set dinner plates *one inch* from the edge of the table. If your plates have a pattern or monogram, set each plate so the design is facing the diner.

Underplates are plates that go *under a dish*, such as a soup bowl or ice cream dish.

Soup plates have a flat rim and are wider and more shallow than a soup bowl.

Coffee or tea cups with saucers or mugs are often included in the place setting for breakfast and brunch, but usually not at lunch, and never at dinner. Coffee or tea may be brought to the table with the teaspoon *on the saucer* at the beginning of the dessert course.

Serveware - bowls, platters, cake stands, and pitchers used for serving food and beverages. Serveware can be made of the finest quality china and porcelain, crystal, copper, pewter, wood, stainless steel, stoneware, earthenware, and plastic.

Glassware - comes in two categories: tumblers (flat bottomed) and stemmed. Glassware types range from plain glass to finer quality crystal glass and are used for drinking specific beverages. See page 65.

Place the water goblet *one inch above the tip of the dinner knife* and the wine glasses to the *right* of the water goblet in order of use. The first used wine glass is placed *furthest* from the water goblet.

When setting the table, take care not to touch the rims of the glassware or the tips of the flatware which would come in contact with a diner's mouth.

Flatware - commonly known as silverware, consists of forks, knives and spoons. Flatware can be made of sterling silver, silverplate, stainless steel or plastic.

Number one table setting rule

> Place flatware on the table in the order it will be used. Flatware used first is on the farthest left and farthest right sides of the plate. Forks are placed on the *left* of the dinner plate and knives and spoons are placed on the *right*. The diner will work from the outside in as the courses are served.

Align bottoms of flatware pieces with the bottom edge of the plate which is one inch from the edge of the table. Flatware should be evenly spaced, starting a half inch from the charger or dinner plate. Avoid placing unnecessary flatware on your table.

A bit of history

Table knives we use today evolved from a somewhat sordid past. In the 1600s, knives with pointed ends proved troublesome for the French court. King Louis XIII's chief minister was so appalled when dinner guests picked their teeth with their table knives, that he had the points ground down. Worse than atrocious manners, was violence. Heated dinner "discussions" often shortened the evening as well as a number of quarrelsome guests' lives. Consequently, King Louis XIV implemented "knife control," outlawing all pointed knives and substituting them with blunt tips.

Forks

Place no more than three forks on the *left* of the place setting. Two exceptions are the cocktail fork and the dessert fork. The cocktail fork is placed to the *outside right* of the knives, resting inside the bowl of the soup spoon, or placed on the *right side* of the underplate when the seafood cocktail is served. The dessert fork may be pre-set *above* the plate or brought to the table on the dessert plate.

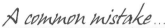

is to set a salad fork as part of the place setting when the salad is served on the same plate as the rest of the dinner.

Example: A salad fork is not necessary when the salad, steak and baked potato are all served on the same plate.

Knives

Place no more than three knives on the *right* of the place setting with the *blade facing* the dinner plate.

Butter spreader knives are placed on top of individual bread and butter plates with the blade facing towards the center of the plate. Choose one of three options:

Spoons

Soup spoons are placed to the *right* of the dinner knife. Round bowled spoons are used for cream soups. Oval-tipped place spoons (often mistakenly called tablespoons) are used for chunky-style soup.

Dessert spoons may be set in three ways ~ pre-set above the dinner plate with the handle pointing to the right ~ pre-set on the left of the dinner knife, next to the dinner plate ~ placed on the right side of the place setting at the beginning of the dessert course after all previous course flatware has been removed. See page 45, The Dessert Course.

Teaspoons, when used for coffee or tea, are placed on the *right* side of the saucer *behind* the coffee cup handle. They may also be placed to the right of the dinner knife, but only if the mug, coffee or tea cup and saucer are part of the place setting for breakfast, brunch or a tea.

is to place a teaspoon on the table when it will not be used for any part of the meal.

Salt and Pepper Shakers

Place salt and pepper shaker sets on the table together. For eight or more guests, place one set at each end of the table. Individual-size salt and pepper shakers or salt cellars and pepper pots may be set on the left side of each place setting or placed between two place settings for two diners to share.

Centerpiece - for decorative purposes; most often placed in the center of the table. Examples: flowers, fruit, art, candles, vines, fir boughs.

Centerpieces should be low enough not to interfere with the diner's view of each other or hinder the serving of the meal. Choose flowers and candles that are non-fragrant so they do not compete with the flavors of the meal. Candlesticks should burn *higher or lower* than the eye level of seated guests. Tall candles create the most flattering light for your guests. They should not be lit until dusk.

Breaking the rule

"Both Linda and I have dining tables that seat eight to ten, but when we have a small number of guests for dinner, we often set the centerpiece at one end of the table. The center between diners is used for platters of food for guests to serve themselves."
~ Rosemarie

Wine Bottle Coasters - used to hold a wine or champagne bottle to protect the table or linens from condensation and drips that stain. Coasters range from four to seven inches wide and come in various heights, shapes and materials.

champagne bottle coaster   wine bottle coaster

Pre-set a coaster for each wine being served. For eight or more guests, pre-set coasters at each end of the table.

Let the Dinner Party Begin

"Dinner is not what you do in the evening before something else. Dinner is the evening."

~ Art Buchwald

Five essentials to determine the formality of your dinner party:
- *Reason for the dinner party*
- *Menu and number of courses*
- *Table setting – linens, flatware, dinnerware and glassware*
- *Ambience – music, flowers, candles*
- *Dress code*

PRE-DINNER BASICS

Cocktails and Hors d'Oeuvres

Set up alcoholic and non-alcoholic beverages, hors d'oeuvres, napkins, cocktail and wine glassware in a *separate area away from the dinner table.* Set more drink glasses than you have guests because glasses have been known to grow legs and walk away, only to be found later in remote areas of the house.

Hors d'oeuvres are bite-sized foods served *before dinner* to sustain the guests during a cocktail hour. Served hot or cold, hors d'oeuvres may be as simple as nuts or olives, or more elaborate with cheese plates and finger foods. Limit the amount of hors d'oeuvres served so that your guests fully enjoy dinner.

Cocktail hour is exactly that – no more than one hour of socializing.

Before Guests are Seated

Pour chilled water (*no ice*) to within *one inch* of the top of the glass. Ice causes condensation, making glasses unattractive and leaving hands and table linens wet. You may choose to place a water pitcher filled with chilled water (no ice) on the table or sideboard for refills.

If the dinner table *has been pre-set* with wine glasses, instruct guests not to bring their wine or cocktail glasses to the dinner table. If the dinner table *has not been pre-set* with wine glasses, instruct your guests to bring their wine glasses, but not cocktail glasses, to the dinner table.

You may serve bread or rolls in a basket which is set on the table or on each bread

and butter plate before guests are seated. Consider pre-warming the bread.

Invite your guests to be seated when the first course is placed on the table or is ready to be served. It's still thought a gracious act of kindness for a gentleman to assist seating the woman to his right or left. Hosts are seated last.

AFTER GUESTS ARE SEATED

Saying Grace or Not

The host decides whether grace will be said. As the host, you may offer grace yourself or ask a guest to say it for you. If you choose the latter, give the guest time to prepare before everyone is seated.

Signaling the Beginning of the Meal

If grace is not said, the host places his or her napkin on their lap to signal the beginning of the meal. Guests follow the host and do the same.

Toasting

Both casual and formal dinners call for a welcoming toast that is made by the host. At casual dinners it may be a simple phrase meaning "enjoy your meal" (such as "bon appétit") and is offered to all guests at the beginning of the meal. After this initial toast any guest may make a toast during the meal. Note that before the dinner concludes, someone should make a toast thanking the host for the dinner party.

At a formal dinner the host will generally stand to get everyone's attention and make a welcome toast to all the guests. Protocol calls for the host to give a toast directed specifically to the guest of honor at the beginning of the dessert course. This brief speech honors the individual, refers to the occasion and why the person is being honored. The guest of honor responds before the dessert course has concluded with a return toast thanking the host for the honor of the dinner and says a few words. At this point, any guest may make a toast.

Toasting Tips

- Get everyone's attention by saying, "I'd like to make a toast" and repeat if necessary – don't signal for guests to be quiet by tapping on a drink glass.
- Make a toast seated or standing.
- Make a toast with alcoholic or non-alcoholic beverages.
- Keep remarks brief and to the point.
- Maintain eye contact with the guest of honor while toasting him or her.

Don't be that guest...

- who makes a toast to the host before the host makes the welcoming toast to all the guests.
- who drinks from your glass immediately after a toast has been made to you – it's like applauding to yourself.
- who raises your glass when a toast is made to you; instead, simply nod your head and smile.

A brief history of the toast

As early as the sixth century B.C., the Greeks toasted to the health of their friends assuring them that the wine they were about to drink wasn't poisoned. The tradition of clinking glasses made a short evening for everyone if poisoned wine splashed from one drink glass to another. Perhaps it was as simple as wanting to bring all five senses into the wine experience – vision, touch, smell, taste – and the clinking sound made by lightly tapping the drinking vessels together added hearing. The Romans added to this custom by dropping a piece of burnt bread into the glass to make poor quality wine more palatable, giving us the word "toast." At some point in history, people began clinking glasses as part of the toast to celebrate their family and friends.

STYLES OF SERVING THE MEAL

Family Style

The main and side dishes are brought to the table in serving bowls, on platters, or a combination of both. The family style of serving means less trips for the host carrying plates from the kitchen. This creates a warm atmosphere around the table and reduces the workload for the host. Foods are *passed to the right*, moving only in one direction between the diners.

Plated Style

Each guest's food is artfully arranged on a plate in the kitchen and brought to the table with no more than one plate in each hand. *Serve to the diner's left*, placing the protein on the plate nearest the diner at the six o'clock position. The guest of honor is served first, if there is one. If no guest of honor, women are served first. When the course is completed, remove *from the diner's right*. Don't be afraid to ask for help in advance. Select a guest whom you know enjoys assisting you.

Butler Style

You don't have to employ a butler to serve your meal butler style. Food, such as a sliced turkey or Beef Wellington, is placed on a large platter with a serving fork. The host or a selected guest carries the platter, circling around the table for all seated guests to serve themselves from the held platter.

Combination of Serving Styles

As a host, you may choose to combine family, plated and butler styles for ease of service or to add a degree of formality to your dinner. Example: Plate the soup in the kitchen and bring it to the seated guests. Serve main course side dishes family style in bowls passed around the table. Serve the main protein item, such as a sliced turkey, butler style from a platter.

Formal Dinner Service

At formal dinners, platters or bowls used for serving are not placed on the table. Food is plated in the kitchen and served to each guest by the course, or selected foods are served butler style on platters for guests to serve themselves. Second helpings are not offered.

BASICS OF SERVING THE MEAL

Serving the Wine

The host chooses when to begin the wine service. Uncork the wine bottles before guests are seated. The wine may be poured beginning with the first course or main course. Wine service with the salad course is tricky. When pairing a salad with wine, take into account the flavors in the wine, salad ingredients and salad dressing. Avoid salad dressings that are too acidic.

Wine is poured after guests are seated. If multiple wines are served, pour each wine with the appropriate food course. Remove the course plate and accompanying wine glass, ideally before the next food course is served. Also have non-alcoholic beverages available, such as sparkling water and ciders.

Wine and all beverages are *poured and removed from the right* side of the diner.

Fill wine glasses with about *four ounces* of wine, but no more than halfway. If you are a couple hosting the party, designate one of you to be responsible for pouring the wine. If hosting alone, appoint someone to assist you with this. When no one is designated to pour the wine, bottles are passed around the table and guests pour for themselves.

About courses

- **Courses are separate parts of the meal served at one time, starting with lighter savory foods and moving toward the heavier main portion of the dinner, and ending with a sweet dessert or a cheese course.**
- **Serve the next course in a timely manner so your guests are not kept waiting.**
- **A dinner party must have a minimum of four courses to be considered formal.**

Appetizers as a First Course

An *appetizer course* is served to *begin the meal at the dinner table*. Its purpose is to stimulate the appetite for the meal to come. Pre-set the necessary flatware for this course on the dinner table or bring in on the plate with the appetizer.

Small but flavorful portions of an appetizer are generally pre-plated on a salad or accent plate and placed on each dinner plate or charger before guests are seated. Suggestions: Fettuccini pasta, mushroom risotto, oysters on the half shell, crab cakes, baked goat cheese and roasted garlic, or baked clams with pesto.

When serving appetizers in tasting spoons, serve three to four tasting spoons per person filled with *bite-sized portions*, such as a small scallop with pesto, a cube of steak with Roquefort cheese sauce, or pasta with butter and capers.

Remove appetizer plate and soiled flatware *from the right* side of the diner before serving the next course.

Salad Course

Serve salad on chilled plates or bowls, especially in hot weather. Chill plates by placing them in the refrigerator earlier in the day. Salad served before the main course is American style. Salad served after the main course is Continental style.

Plated style: Salad plates are filled in the kitchen with a prepared salad and dressing. Place salad plate on top of the dinner plate or charger before guests are seated. This helps control salad portions so the host doesn't run short of salad for everyone.

Family style: Set empty salad plates on top of the dinner plates or chargers before guests are seated. Pre-set the salad serving bowl with salad tongs or a salad serving fork and spoon on the table just prior to the guests being seated. The host begins by holding the salad bowl for the person to his or her right for the guest to serve herself. The next person repeats the process of holding the salad bowl for the diner to the right, until it reaches the host who is served last.

When everyone has finished eating the salad course, *remove* the salad plates and soiled flatware from the *right of the diner*.

Soup Course

To keep soup hot longer, warm the soup bowls first before filling. Four easy ways to warm bowls: run them under hot water and towel dry; stack microwavable bowls and place in a microwave oven for 30-60 seconds; place them in a low temperature oven or run them through the heat cycle in a dishwasher.

Soup plates or soup bowls always have an underplate to prevent soiling the table linens, and makes transporting the soup bowls to the table easier to handle.

Option one: Soup may be filled in a soup plate or soup bowl in the kitchen before placing on top of the dinner plate prior to guests being seated.

Option two: Soup may be served from a soup tureen on the table with a stack of soup plates or bowls sitting beside the tureen. The host fills the bowls which are then *passed to the right*, halfway around the table. Next, the host passes filled bowls to the remaining guests on the left. Host is served last.

Avoid filling soup plates or bowls to the rim.

After guests have finished their soup, *remove* the empty soup plates or bowls from the *diner's right* and take them to the kitchen. Depending on how you plan to serve the main course (either family style or plated) determines whether you remove the dinner plate with the soup plates or bowls or whether the dinner plate remains in place.

Fish Course

The fish course may be a small piece of salmon, halibut or other fish fillet with a sauce, and brought to the guests on a dinner plate. No other foods would be on the plate. Most often the fish course is plated in the kitchen, or served butler style on a platter for guests to serve themselves. *Remove* fish course plate and soiled flatware from the *right side of the diner* before serving the next course.

Sorbet Course

A sorbet course is served after the fish course to cleanse and refresh the palate for the main course. Place a small serving of sorbet in a cordial or liqueur glass with an underplate and a small spoon, such as a demitasse, resting on right side of the underplate. Diners eat a few bites of the sorbet, but do not eat all of it. *Remove* sorbet glass, underplate and soiled flatware from the *right side of the diner* before serving the next course.

Main Course

The previous courses build up to the main course, which is the focal point of your dinner. It usually consists of a protein, starch and a vegetable. The main course may be served plated style with the foods placed and garnished on dinner plates in the kitchen and brought to the table. When placing the dinner plate in front of the diner, rotate the plate so the protein is in the six o'clock position. The main course may also be served family style or a combination of family style and butler style. *Remove* dinner plate and soiled flatware from the *right side of the diner* before serving the next course.

Prior to the dessert course

Remove the charger *if it hasn't been previously removed* and clear the table of all bread and butter plates, salt and pepper shaker sets and any *used* glassware (water glass and champagne glass excluded).

Dessert Course

Option one: Bring dessert, such as cake or pie, and a stack of dessert plates to the table. The host slices individual pieces of dessert and places them on dessert plates. Plates are passed to the diners, *moving around the table to the right*. Host is served last.

Option two: Pre-slice dessert and place on dessert plates in the kitchen, bring to the table and *serve to the left* of each diner.

Option three: Served as a pre-plated dessert in another area such as your living room.

Word to the wise: Place the point of a piece of pie or cake towards the diner.

Beverages served with the dessert course may include a choice of coffee, tea, port, champagne or dessert wines.

THE END OF THE MEAL

The host will remove the napkin from his or her lap and drape it to the left of the place setting. Guests are expected to do the same.

After dessert, hosts may invite guests to join them in another location in the home. As the evening winds down, guests will recirculate with other guests. An option is to serve after-dinner chocolates or mints, espresso, coffee, liqueurs or cordials.

The Party's Over

It is appropriate for guests to stay one hour after the dinner has concluded to avoid "eating and running." Often the last hour or two of the evening is when the host truly gets to enjoy the guests' company.

Don't be that guest...

- who overstays your welcome.
- who drinks too much alcohol.
- who forgets to thank your hosts for a wonderful dinner before saying goodnight.

"Save the Date Cards" and Invitations

RSVP (répondez s'il vous plait) is a French expression which means "please respond" whether or not you will be attending.

Please Save the Date
Thursday, December 31, 2015

Celebration dinner
Mr. and Mrs. Donald Kingsborough
San Francisco
Invitation to follow

"SAVE THE DATE CARDS"

You may send "Save the Date" cards three to six months in advance of your event so that your guests will not make other engagements and will have ample time to make travel and accommodation arrangements.

INVITATIONS

INFORMAL OR CASUAL INVITATIONS

An informal or casual request asking for the presence of guests to attend an event such as a 50th birthday or a college graduation dinner party. Be creative!

Informal and casual invitation protocol

- The style, paper and design of your invitation sets the tone of your dining event.
- Clearly communicate the details of your event, including dress code.
- Date may be written to include numbers: Saturday, December 31st.
- Use A.M. or P.M. to state the time: 7 to 9 P.M.
- Place RSVP information on the invitation; ask for dietary restrictions.
- They may be printed professionally, printed on your computer, handwritten, made by telephone, emailed or produced through website templates.

FORMAL INVITATIONS

A request from the host asking guests for their presence at a formal event such as a wedding dinner in your home or a black tie holiday dinner.

Formal invitation protocol

- Print only on quality paper.
- Use the template shown on the right of this page to state the event information.
- Write out dates: Thursday, December thirty-first.
- Use "o'clock" to state the hour: seven o'clock.
- Handwrite or calligraph envelopes; they may also be printed in the same font as the invitation.
- Send formal invitations four to six weeks in advance.
- Never invite guests to a formal dinner by telephone, email or text message.
- Enclose a RSVP card; ask for dietary restrictions.

HOST
Farys Hixson
EVENT
Dinner Party
WHEN
Tuesday, June 6th at 6:30 P.M.
WHERE
Location Name
RSVP: email@email.com by May 24th
555-123-1234
Dressy casual
Please state dietary restrictions

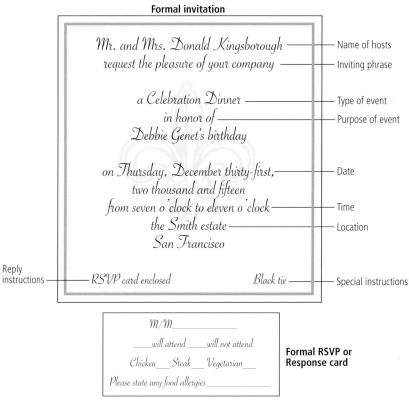

Mr. and Mrs. Donald Kingsborough —— Name of hosts
request the pleasure of your company —— Inviting phrase

a Celebration Dinner —— Type of event
in honor of —— Purpose of event
Debbie Genet's birthday

on Thursday, December thirty-first, —— Date
two thousand and fifteen
from seven o'clock to eleven o'clock —— Time
the Smith estate —— Location
San Francisco

Reply instructions —— *RSVP card enclosed*   *Black tie* —— Special instructions

M/M_____
____will attend ____will not attend
Chicken___ Steak___ Vegetarian___
Please state any food allergies_____

Formal RSVP or Response card

Menu Cards, Place Cards and Thank You Notes

"The people sitting around my table are far more important than the food sitting on their plates."

~ Unknown

MENU CARDS

Menu cards are an extra touch that transform a simple dining experience into an unforgettable one. They may be handwritten, printed on a computer, or written in calligraphy in black ink. Menu cards list each course and may include the wines served. Exclude palate-cleansing sorbets and breads. The date, location and purpose of the dinner may be listed on the top or bottom of the card. Encourage your guests to take the menu cards as a memento of your dinner party.

Menu Card Placement Options: on top of the napkin ~ middle of the plate ~ to the left of the forks ~ leaning against the stem of the water glass ~ just above the middle of the plate.

Menu card with wine pairing

Menu

Cream of mushroom soup
Emilio Lustau VORS Sherry 1980

Grilled Chinook salmon
with dill sauce
Mer Soleil Chardonnay 2009

Mixed greens and brie
with herbed vinaigrette

Beef Wellington
roasted red potatoes
grilled asparagus
Far Niente Cabernet Sauvignon 2007

Baked Alaska
Cristal Champagne 1998

Eugene, Oregon
August 16, 2015

Combination menu card and place card

Calder McWhinney

Menu

Warm goat cheese
with Nicoise olives
and roasted garlic

Roasted pork loin
with mango chutney
mashed sweet potatoes
herbed green beans

Apple pie à la mode

Assorted cheeses and fruit

Danville, California
May 24, 2015

PLACE CARDS AND SEATING ARRANGEMENTS

Place card - a small card with a guest name at each place setting, indicating where each person is to sit. Place cards may be handwritten or printed on a computer.

Kathleen

If your dinner party has both a host and co-host, they sit one at each end of the table. If there is more than one table, the hosts sit at different tables.

Seat the guest of honor to the right of the host. At family gatherings it is nice to give grandparents or the eldest relative a place of honor seating.

Use place cards for eight or more guests. In a private home hosts do not have a place card. Try to seat people together who share common interests, and alternate genders when possible for an interesting mix of conversation.

For a dinner party of friends, use first names only on the place cards. When you have two people with the same first name, use both first and last names. If guests don't know each other, use first and last names.

For a formal dinner party, use only surnames on the place card such as Dr. Pedersen or Mr. Harvey. If you have two Ms. Smiths, you must use their full names on their place cards. If you have two Mr. Jack Burns, include a middle initial when there is no suffix, such as Jr. or Sr. Write place card names in calligraphy or handwrite in black ink only.

Place Card Placement Options: on top of the napkin ~ middle of the plate ~ on the table above the dessert forks ~ leaning against the stem of the water glass ~ above the middle of the plate on the table. It may also be combined with table favors.

Place card arrangements combined with table favors

Only the host can rearrange place cards

- If you are a guest, look for your place card. If there isn't one, wait for your host to indicate where you are to sit.

- At large or formal dinners look for an envelope with your name, indicating where you are to be seated – generally found on an entrance table.

- Once seated, put your place card above the dinner plate or charger.

- Never rearrange your assigned place card seating to suit yourself.

GUEST THANK YOU NOTES

A thank you note is sent to the host of a dining event you attended expressing your appreciation for the invitation, your enjoyment of the meal and the experience.

Must do!
- Telephone, email or text the following day of a dining event.
- Elevate yourself by following up with a handwritten thank you note card.

The elements of a well-written thank you note
- Thank the person for the dining experience.
- Add a personal touch, such as complimenting the table settings.
- Mention an item from the menu that you especially enjoyed.
- Express how much you enjoyed the evening. Thank the host for including you.

January 5, 2015

Dear Connie and Sean,
Thank you for the over-the-top dinner last night. Connie, your table settings were stunning, and the salted caramel favors never made it home. Delicious! The food was spectacular, especially Sean's prime rib. We enjoyed meeting your friends who were very funny and entertaining. You always make everyone feel so welcome and at ease. Thanks again for including us in your wonderful New Year's Eve dinner. Next time it's our turn!

Love,
Sloane and Sim

Manners $Simply$™

PREPARING THE TABLE

- Place all *liquids* (drink glasses) *on the right* of the place setting.

- Place *solids* (bread) *on the left* of the place setting.

- Pre-butter the toast for a casual breakfast. Slice in half, place stack of toast on a serving plate and bring to the table.

- Fill the coffee mug, juice or milk glass three-fourths of the way full.

Napkin finesse

- In a private home, wait until the host has removed the napkin from his or her place setting before removing yours.

- Remove napkin ring and place it to the left of your plate.

- As you place the napkin on your lap, unfold it below the level of the table, folding it in half so the crease faces your waistline.

- Use your napkin throughout the meal to blot your lips and wipe your fingers.

- Pick up your napkin if it falls from your lap. If not retrievable, ask your host for another one.

- Place napkin on your chair if you need to excuse yourself before the end of the meal.

- Drape your napkin loosely and place it to the left side of the place setting at the end of the meal.

Don't be that guest...

- who tucks your napkin into your shirt or trousers.

- who blows your nose in your napkin, whether it is cloth or paper.

- who wads your napkin and then leaves it on your dinner plate.

Create Your Own Breakfast

This place setting is perfect for:

▸ On-the-run breakfast

▸ Overnight guest
  simple breakfast

▸ Saturday breakfast

Starting with Breakfast

MENU: HOT STEEL-CUT OATS WITH BROWN SUGAR AND DRIED CRANBERRIES, BUTTERED TOAST, FRESH SQUEEZED ORANGE JUICE, COFFEE

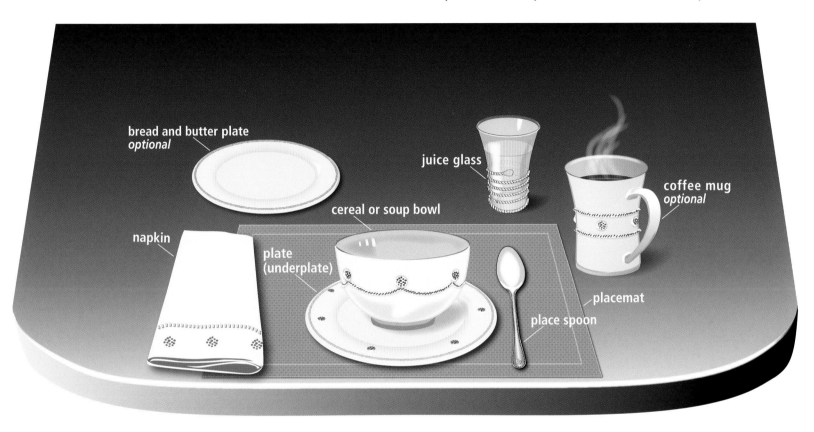

DINING TIPS

▸ Rest your spoon on the underplate between bites.

▸ Place breakfast bread on the bread and butter plate or underplate between bites. Rest flatware on the underplate while taking a bite of bread. Avoid holding bread in one hand and your flatware in your other hand at the same time.

▸ Do not apply butter and jam to a biscuit and put it back together to eat sandwich style.

Manners Simply™

PREPARING THE TABLE

The Everyday Breakfast, Lunch or Dinner place setting on the opposite page is a perfect table setting to begin teaching children how to set the table. Involve the whole family. Some may help prepare the meal, some serve, and others set the table and clear dishes.

Where's the teaspoon?

Do not use a teaspoon as part of the place setting unless a spoon is required for use in any part of the meal. See page 12.

Remember what your mother told you

- Sit up straight.

- Rest both feet flat on the floor. Do not twist your legs around the legs of the chair. You may cross your legs at the ankle.

- Keep elbows off the table when eating.

- Do not start eating until everyone else has been served, unless instructed by the host.

- Say "please" when asking for something to be passed to you and "thank you" once you receive it.

- Do not talk or chew with your mouth full.

- Eat quietly. Do not smack your lips while eating.

- Take small bites. Do not overload your mouth.

Create Your Own Everyday Breakfast, Lunch or Dinner

This place setting is perfect for:
- ▶ Time out for yourself breakfast
- ▶ Let's do lunch
- ▶ Typical family dinner

Everyday Breakfast, Lunch or Dinner
a place setting your child or grandchild can master

BREAKFAST MENU: OLD FASHIONED PANCAKES WITH BLUEBERRY SYRUP
LUNCH MENU: BLACK BEAN AND AVOCADO SALAD, CRUSTY FRENCH BREAD
DINNER MENU: ZOV'S FAVORITE MEATLOAF, BUTTERMILK MASHED POTATOES, SAUTÉED SWISS CHARD WITH LEMON AND PINE NUTS

DINING TIPS

▸ When unsure what to do once you sit down at the table, follow the lead of the host. Don't dive in and start to serve yourself or, worse yet, begin to eat.

▸ Ask for food to be passed, rather than reaching across the table.

▸ Do not cut all your food on your plate at once.

▸ Try a bite of everything served to you, unless you are allergic to the food.

Manners Simply™

PREPARING THE TABLE

Brunch is a combination of breakfast and lunch, usually served mid to late morning.

- Pour chilled water (*no ice*) before guests are seated. Ice causes condensation on the outside of the glass, making it unattractive and messy.

- A jam jar or pot for condiments like jam or lemon curd may be placed on the table with or without an underplate. If you don't have a jam jar, use a small dish with an underplate such as a salad plate. Place a jelly spoon or small spoon on the underplate for guests to use to serve themselves. Guests will remove breakfast condiments (jam or lemon curd) from a container and place on their bread and butter plate. If one is not provided, condiments may be placed on the dinner plate.

jam jar or pot

Coffee and Tea Service

For ease of service, a coffee server or teapot may be set on the table, possibly on a warmer or in a thermal carafe.

A sugar and creamer set may be placed on the table for the coffee or tea. If you are serving granulated sugar in the sugar bowl, provide a sugar serving spoon for all diners to use. Provide sugar tongs when sugar lumps or sugar cubes are served. If serving eight or more guests, place a sugar and creamer set at each end of the table.

A bit of napkin ring history

In the early 1800s, napkin rings were originally made of silver and imprinted with the names of the family member allowing them to identify their own napkin between wash days.

Create Your Own
Breakfast or Brunch

This place setting is perfect for:
- Mother's Day brunch
- Romantic brunch for two
- Ladies who brunch

Weekend Breakfast or Brunch

MENU: RUBY RED GRAPEFRUIT, BUTTERMILK BISCUITS,
SPANISH OMELET WITH MANCHEGO CHEESE, GRILLED ASPARAGUS, MIMOSAS, COFFEE OR TEA

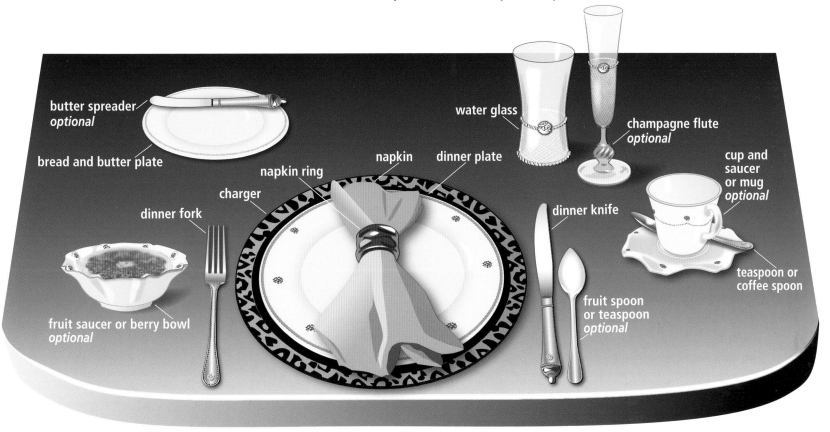

DINING TIPS

▸ Hold your coffee or tea cup by the handle. Do not cradle in your hands as you might with a mug.

▸ Just say, "No, thank you" if you do not wish to be served coffee or tea. Do not turn the cup upside down.

▸ Once a piece of flatware is used it remains on the plate and no part of the flatware touches the tabletop again.

▸ Do not push your plate away from you.
Use the "I'm finished" position when finishing any course.

Silent Signal
"I'm finished with this course or meal."

Manners Simply™

PREPARING THE TABLE

Salad fork confusion?

Although it is correct to set both a salad and a dinner fork when serving salad on the side, it is equally correct and more efficient to set only a dinner fork. When serving a One-Course Casual Lunch or Dinner, diners use the dinner fork for both salad and main course.

No labels on the table

When serving bottled salad dressing, sour cream, ketchup, mustard or other condiments, avoid putting store-bought containers on the table. Instead use an attractive bottle or bowl with a spoon or ladle. Picnics and casual backyard barbecues are an exception. You may even call it a "labels on the table party."

Are you this guest?

"I was planning a birthday party and when several guests called to RSVP, they asked if they could bring a food item to the dinner. The answer was always the same 'No, thank you. Just bring your smiling faces.' I had cooked beans all day long and had purchased a special birthday cake to serve with ice cream. When the guests arrived, two brought flowers, causing me to rush around to find vases. Another two guests each brought dessert, and a fifth guest brought beans. After I bit my tongue in restraint, I served all the food items that had been brought, including my own."

~ Mary Anne

Tips

- Don't bring food to a dinner without coordinating with the host. Honor their wishes if they say not to bring a contributing food item.

- Do bring a host gift, such as a bottle of wine, a scented candle, or flowers in a vase with a tag identifying you as the gift giver.

- Flowers may be sent in advance of the dinner party or as a thank you gift after the party.

Create Your Own Casual Lunch or Dinner

This place setting is perfect for:
- ▶ Friends connecting for lunch
- ▶ Unexpected guests dinner
- ▶ After golf or bocce dinner

One-Course Casual Lunch or Dinner
with salad on the side

LUNCH OR DINNER MENU: SPAGHETTI WITH TURKEY MEATBALLS AND MARINARA SAUCE, GARLIC BREAD, MIXED GREEN SALAD

DINING TIPS

▸ Pass *food* counter-clockwise, *moving from the left to the right*. Food only moves in one direction.

▸ Cut off a pat of butter from the cube with your unused dinner knife and place on the dinner plate if a butter knife is not available.

▸ Place bread on the rim of your dinner plate if there's no bread and butter plate.

▸ When bread is passed and slices are not cut all the way through, use the cloth lining the basket as a buffer to hold the bread in place with one hand. Pull off the slice with your other hand.

PREPARING THE TABLE

- Serve cream soups, such as lobster bisque or cream of mushroom, in a cream soup bowl.

- Generally chunky-style soups, such as roasted tomato with eggplant or minestrone, are served in a flat-rimmed soup plate.

- Large soup or cereal bowls may be used for a one-dish meal such as chili or stew.

- Set round bowled soup spoons for cream soups. Set oval-tipped place spoons, often mistakenly called a tablespoon, when serving a chunky-style of soup.

Garnishing your soup - a nice touch!

Family style: Place garnishes in a sectioned condiment dish or small bowls with appropriate size serving utensils for guests to serve themselves. An option is to place all the condiment bowls on a tray or plate so they may be passed at the same time.

Plated style: Host garnishes each bowl of soup in the kitchen, before serving guests the soup course.

Garnish options: croutons, cheese, crème fraîche or sour cream with fresh herbs such as basil, chives or parsley.

A fun and easy way to serve soup

"I was hosting a boat parade dinner party when an unexpected weather change turned a balmy southern California evening into a 'dark and stormy night.' Thinking quickly, I switched a planned cold hors d'oeuvre to a hot soup and grabbed several boxes of tomato bisque from the pantry. Each guest received a warm mug of soup topped with a splash of sherry wine and crème fraîche as they stepped outside onto the dock. Served in this way, no flatware was required. The soup helped to keep my guests warm, and they loved it. This was the beginning of an annual tradition."

~ Rosemarie

Create Your Own Two- or Three-Course Dinner

This place setting is perfect for:

- ▸ Sunday family dinner
- ▸ My in-laws are coming to dinner
- ▸ It's a cold night dinner with the new neighbors

Two- or Three-Course Dinner
beginning with soup

FIRST COURSE SOUP MINESTRONE, DINNER ROLLS
SECOND COURSE MAIN ROSEMARY GARLIC CHICKEN WITH LEMON, RISOTTO WITH FRESH PEAS, MUSHROOMS AND CORN
THIRD COURSE DESSERT JASMINE RICE PUDDING WITH FRESH BERRIES *OPTIONAL*

water goblet

wine glass

bread and butter plate
optional

placemat

dinner fork

soup plate

dinner plate

dinner knife

napkin

place or soup spoon

DINING TIPS

▸ Sip the soup quietly, without slurping.

▸ Lean forward slightly, filling the soup spoon about three-fourths full. *Spoon away from yourself* while skimming your spoon across the top where the soup is cooler. Gently touch the back rim of the bowl with the bottom of your spoon to remove any drips. *Do not blow on your soup as a way to cool it.*

▸ Tip the bowl away from yourself, using your soup spoon to get the last of the soup.

▸ The spoon remains in the soup plate when pausing or finished with your soup. The spoon is placed on the underplate of the soup bowl when pausing or finished with your soup.

Soup Plate Silent Signal
"I'm pausing between bites"
and "I'm finished."

Soup Bowl Silent Signal
"I'm pausing between bites"
and "I'm finished."

PREPARING THE TABLE

- Inform guests that dinner will begin in approximately 10-15 minutes so they may finish their hors d'oeuvres and drinks. Instruct guests to leave their glassware in the cocktail area. If you're short on wine glasses, ask guests to bring their wine glass to the table. Use these last minutes to plate the first course or add touches to the table, such as lighting the candles.

- Attractive serving dishes or platters enhance the appearance of your table and appeal of the food.

- *Clear the dishes* from the table *two at a time*, one in each hand. Never scrape food from the plates at the table or stack them before removing.

Everyone has had a dinner gone wrong

"I was about to serve a multi-course dinner for eight. My guests and I were in the living room having cocktails and hors d'oeuvres while the prime rib roast was resting on the kitchen counter. The guests were raving about how good it smelled and were eagerly waiting for dinner to be served. I invited everyone to be seated at the table and went to carve the roast, only to find it missing. My dog, Ralph, was happily dining on the roast under the kitchen table, enjoying every bite. After quietly panicking, I laughingly announced that we were about to have a menu change. We poured more wine, ordered a pizza and had a great time."

~ Rosemarie

Create Your Own Two- or Three-Course Dinner

This place setting is perfect for:

▸ Celebration dinner, birthday, promotion, retirement

▸ Guys' night out

▸ Girls just want to have fun

Two- or Three-Course Dinner
beginning with salad

FIRST COURSE SALAD ROMAINE WITH HEARTS OF PALM AND ARTICHOKES, RUSTIC ARTISAN BREAD
SECOND COURSE MAIN SIMPLE POACHED SALMON, GARLIC ROASTED CAULIFLOWER, RICE PILAF WITH LENTILS AND CARAMELIZED ONIONS
THIRD COURSE DESSERT CHERRY CRISP *OPTIONAL*

DINING TIPS

▶ Break off only one bite-sized piece of bread at a time. Butter it on the plate, not in your hand or mid-air.

▶ Remove non-edible objects, such as fish bones, olive pits, gristle or fat, with your fingers or flatware and place them on the edge of your plate.

▶ Place personal items like eye glasses, cell phone or small purse away from the table top.

▶ Texting or talking on your cell phone is not appropriate during the meal.

Manners Simply™

PREPARING THE TABLE
Did you know that…?

- an appetizer course is served to *begin the meal at the dinner table*. Its purpose is to stimulate the appetite for the meal to come. On the other hand, hors d'oeuvres are bite-sized foods served *before dinner away from the dinner table* to sustain the guests during a cocktail hour.

- tasting spoons contain one bite-sized portion in each spoon so diners may enjoy a variety of foods. You can assemble tasting spoons on an appetizer plate and pre-set as a first course at each place setting just before guests are seated.

- table favors are a gift of appreciation for guests who are attending your dinner party. You may attach a place card to a table favor such as a wrapped truffle, nuts, a small jar of jam, or holiday ornaments. Pre-set table favors on or above the dinner plate or charger before guests are seated.

- a party cracker isn't a fancy saltine, but rather a decorative party favor that holds candy or small collectables. It pops when a paper strip is pulled at one or both ends of the party cracker and torn apart. It is opened prior to, or after, dessert.

A dinner to remember

"For my birthday I always celebrate by creating a daring menu, inviting all those who mean a lot to me. I plan every detail, experimenting with new cuisines and themes. My guests eagerly look forward to this culinary experience as they know they will be treated to a meal that is truly ADVENTUROUS!"

~ Kathy

Create Your Own
Adventurous Affair

This place setting is perfect for:
- Food lovers' dinner
- Expressing your creative side
- Having the kind of affair you *want* people to talk about

Three-Course Adventurous Affair
beginning with appetizer

FIRST COURSE BITE-SIZED APPETIZERS CHOPPED TOMATO, OLIVE, MOZZARELLA CHEESE; SUSHI TOPPED WITH CAVIAR; ANGEL HAIR PASTA AND MARINARA SAUCE
SECOND COURSE MAIN ROASTED GOAT WITH RED WINE REDUCTION SAUCE, RED POTATOES, SAUTÉED BROCCOLINI
THIRD COURSE DESSERT KATAIFI WITH RICOTTA CUSTARD AND ORANGE BLOSSOM SYRUP

DINING TIPS

▸ Pick up a tasting spoon and eat the appetizer in one bite. Do not pick up the food with your fingers from the tasting spoon. Return empty tasting spoon to the appetizer plate.

▸ Taste your food before adding salt. By salting it first, you are assuming that the flavors need enhancement, but the taste could already be perfect!

▸ Resist the temptation to ask for condiments, such as steak sauce, ketchup or hot sauce. It's considered rude and suggests the host hasn't used the proper seasoning on a dish that may have taken hours to prepare.

Manners Simply™

PREPARING THE TABLE

- Place individual salt shaker to the right side of the pepper shaker because most people are right-handed and use more salt than pepper.

- Setting a bread and butter plate at each place setting allows guests to separate their bread from other foods on a dinner plate that may have sauces, gravy or juices.

- Pre-set a chilled butter pat on the lower right-hand side of the bread and butter plate just before guests are seated. For a creative touch, check with your local retailer or online for specialty butter pat molds, such as leaves for an autumn dinner.

Early guests

"Many years ago I was hosting a barbecue for 70 people at my new home. Two hours before the party started, my first guests arrived. I hadn't showered and dressed yet and was still in the last-minute clean-up mode. When the guests asked 'What can we do to help you?' I didn't hesitate. I said 'You can clean the toilets.' They never came early again."

~ Linda

How the French do it

In French homes, a mixed green salad is often served after the main course. One way to have the salad ready to go is to prepare it before dinner starts, layering it in the salad bowl so the dressing is at the bottom of the bowl, with the torn greens on top. Toss just before serving.

~ *from Everyday Cooking with Organic Produce by Cathy Thomas*

Create Your Own Fabulous Affair

This place setting is perfect for:
- Valentine's Day or holiday dinner
- Date night
- Engagement dinner

Four-Course Fabulous Affair

FIRST COURSE SOUP GOLDEN LENTIL, FLAT BREAD • **SECOND COURSE SALAD** TUSCANY TOMATO WITH KALAMATA OLIVES
THIRD COURSE MAIN BEEF TENDERLOIN WITH SPINACH, LEEKS, GOAT CHEESE, YUKON GOLD O'BRIEN POTATOES
FOURTH COURSE DESSERT CARAMELIZED APPLES WITH COGNAC AND VANILLA ICE CREAM

DINING TIPS

▸ Pass the salt and pepper shakers together. This applies even if a fellow diner asks for either the salt or pepper shaker.

▸ Ask your host for a replacement if you drop a flatware piece on the floor.

▸ Do not arrive early to a dinner party, and out of respect to your host, arrive no more than 15 minutes late. If you are running late, notify the host of your scheduled arrival time.

PREPARING THE TABLE

Continental (European) style dining differs from American style dining in two ways: when the salad is served and how the flatware is held. See page 59 for holding flatware Continental and American style.

In Continental style dining, the *salad is served after* the main course. Therefore, the salad fork is placed to the *right of the dinner fork,* and the salad knife is placed to the *left of the dinner knife*.

- Place small individual salt and pepper shakers to the left of each place setting or between two place settings for two diners to share.

- Place the wine bottle on a wine coaster to avoid staining the tablecloth. Or better yet, pour the wine into a decanter. A decanter, used to aerate and separate the sediment from the wine, will not leave a mark on a wooden table or on a table linen.

Good to know

- When planning your menu, not everything has to be over-the-top. Select one menu item to be memorable.

- A fish course would consist solely of a small piece of fish with a sauce (for example, salmon with a dill sauce).

- When serving four courses or more, the portions of food per course is smaller.

- Do not ruin your meal by waiting for late guests. If guests arrive late, serve them the same course the others are eating.

Create Your Own Stately Affair

This place setting is often used at the White House for official dinners. It is also perfect for:

- ▶ Semi-formal or formal dinner
- ▶ Fundraiser dinner
- ▶ International guest dinner

Four-Course Stately Affair
set Continental style

FIRST COURSE FISH PAN SEARED WHITE FISH WITH TOMATO CURRY SAUCE
SECOND COURSE MAIN BEEF TENDERLOIN WITH SHALLOT AND THYME SAUCE ON A BED OF BRAISED SPINACH, CREAMY MASHED POTATOES
THIRD COURSE SALAD BEET SALAD WITH WATERCRESS
FOURTH COURSE DESSERT SIMPLE POACHED PEARS

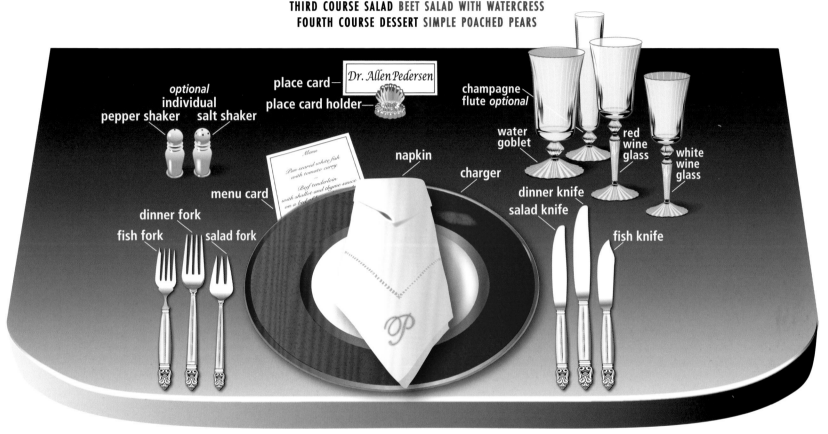

DINING TIPS

▸ Return your glassware to the upper right side of the place setting after each use.

▸ Cut one small bite of meat at a time – Continental style.
   Cut one to three small bites of meat at a time – American style.

▸ Do not use a back-and-forth motion to saw your way through the meat.

Manners Simply™

PREPARING THE TABLE
Did you know that…?

- no food is served directly on a charger or a service plate.

- a salt spoon may be placed in the salt cellar up to a few hours before guests arrive, or a salt spoon may lie on the right side of the salt cellar. Keep in mind that salt is corrosive to silver and will eventually cause black spots or pitting if left in contact with silver over long periods of time.

- salt and pepper shakers, bread and butter plates, butter spreaders and chargers are *removed before the dessert course is served*.

A nice touch

After a prawn appetizer course that guests have eaten with their fingers, pass a tray filled with warm, rolled, damp towels along with slices of lemon. Guests squeeze a little lemon juice on the towel and gently wipe their fingers to remove the fish odors. Pass a tray or basket for collection of towels and lemon.

Hint to warm towels: place damp, white terry cloth washcloths in the microwave for a few seconds.

A surprise wedding

"Consider having a garden-wedding dinner party using this five-course place setting. I did. Starting with the first course, we dined at our family table. Each of the other tables was set with two empty place settings, set on opposite sides of the table. After each course, we moved to another table to dine so we could visit with each of our surprised guests. Most didn't know they were coming to a wedding!"
~ Linda

Create Your Own Sophisticated Affair

This place setting is perfect for:
- ▸ Pre-Christmas dinner with friends
- ▸ New Year's Eve dinner
- ▸ Murder mystery game dinner

Five-Course Sophisticated Affair
set Continental style

FIRST COURSE APPETIZER PRAWNS WITH COCKTAIL SAUCE • **SECOND COURSE SOUP** PUREÉ OF BUTTERNUT SQUASH, DINNER ROLLS
THIRD COURSE MAIN ROASTED RACK OF LAMB WITH POMEGRANATE SAUCE, POTATO GRATIN, HERBED GREEN BEANS • **FOURTH COURSE SALAD** GREEK SALAD
FIFTH COURSE DESSERT BREAD PUDDING WITH CHOCOLATE CHUNKS AND BANANAS

DINING TIPS

*Flatware is arranged by order of use. Pieces furthest from the dinner plate are used first.
Work from the outside in when beginning to dine.*

▸ Pick up the prawn by its tail using your fingers. Dip in sauce and eat in two or more bites.
  Discard the tails onto the underplate, not on the charger.

▸ When a salt cellar has no salt spoon, you may take a pinch of salt with your fingers or
  use the tip of your dinner knife to transfer the salt to your food.

Manners Simply™

PREPARING THE TABLE

- If space is limited, move wine glasses closer together or overlap them when setting the table.

- Pour each wine with the appropriate food course. When that food course plate is removed, remove the accompanying wine glass, ideally before the next food course is served.

- *Pour and remove* wine and all beverages from the *right* side of the diner.

Table talk

It's a good indication that you've been monopolizing the conversation if you see others are halfway through their dinner and your plate is full.

Dinner mishap

"Guests were seating themselves at the dinner table while I was in the kitchen, preparing the serving bowls and platters. I had garlic mashed potatoes warming in the oven. In a hurried rush, my hand slipped off the pot holder and I burned my hand. The pot landed upside-down on the floor. My sole witness helped me scoop up the contents which hadn't touched the floor. We put the potatoes in the serving bowl and delivered it to the table. Until now, we've kept our secret."

~ Linda

Create Your Own Formal Affair

This place setting is perfect for:

- ▶ Black or white tie formal dinner
- ▶ Wine and food pairing dinner
- ▶ Formal dinner on your private yacht

Six-Course Formal Affair
set Continental style

FIRST COURSE APPETIZER MIXED SEAFOOD COCKTAIL • **SECOND COURSE SOUP** VELVETY CREAM OF SPINACH AND CAULIFLOWER
THIRD COURSE FISH STUFFED TROUT WITH TAHINI SAUCE • **FOURTH COURSE MAIN** PHYLLO PURSES WITH CHICKEN AND CARAMELIZED ONIONS, HERBED POTATOES
FIFTH COURSE SALAD MEDITERRANEAN CHOP SALAD
SIXTH COURSE DESSERT APPLE CINNAMON PHYLLO CRUMBLE WITH ICE CREAM

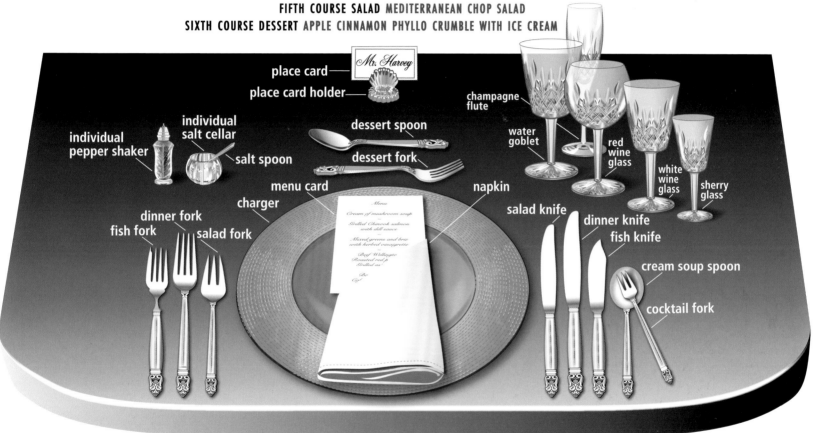

DINING TIPS

▸ Once seated, tuck the menu card slightly under the charger for reference throughout the meal.

▸ Pour a *splash* of sherry on top of the soup and drink the remainder from your sherry glass.

▸ *Pace yourself* with the other diners. Don't eat too quickly or too slowly.

▸ Do not apply lipstick or use a toothpick at the table. Excuse yourself quietly, place your napkin on the seat of your chair and do your personal grooming in private.

Manners Simply™

PREPARING THE TABLE

American style dining differs from Continental style dining in two ways: when the salad is served and how the flatware is held. See page 59 for holding flatware American and Continental style.

In American style dining the *salad is served before* the main course. Therefore, the salad fork is placed to the *left of the dinner fork*, and the salad knife is placed to the *right of the dinner knife* in American formal dining.

- The *only time* you set a fork on the right side of the place setting is when serving a seafood cocktail appetizer.

- Framed menu cards are often given to guests as a table favor. At the end of your dinner party, announce to the guests this special menu card is theirs to take home.

A bit of history

Traditionally, soup was eaten as the first course and the nuts were eaten after the dessert course. This gave rise to the saying "from soup to nuts," meaning from start to finish.

Be creative!

"I turned a formal event into a shared cooking extravaganza.

"I invited guests who were fun and adventurous, asking them to arrive early and to bring aprons. I greeted them with chilled champagne and hors d'oeuvres. Each guest picked a recipe card out of a bowl. Some cards were duplicated for complicated dishes that required more than one chef. They found the spot in my kitchen where I had all the necessary ingredients for their recipe. Very soon everyone was laughing, chopping, mixing, baking, peeling and grating until everything from appetizers to dessert was prepared. Each of the chefs was responsible for plating, garnishing and serving their part of the meal. This was a great way to lighten up a formal affair and turn it into an unforgettable dinner party."

~ Rosemarie

Create Your Own Formal Affair

This place setting is perfect for:

- ▸ Black or white tie formal dinner
- ▸ Downton Abbey dinner
- ▸ Dining until midnight on New Year's Eve

Six-Course Formal Affair
set American style

FIRST COURSE APPETIZER CRAB COCKTAIL • **SECOND COURSE SOUP** CREAM OF MUSHROOM TOPPED WITH SHERRY
THIRD COURSE FISH GRILLED SWORDFISH WITH TOMATOES, OLIVES • **FOURTH COURSE SALAD** ENDIVE WITH WALNUTS AND CHAMPAGNE DRESSING
FIFTH COURSE MAIN DUCK CONFIT, WILD RICE, ROASTED BRUSSELS SPROUTS
SIXTH COURSE DESSERT BAKED ALASKA

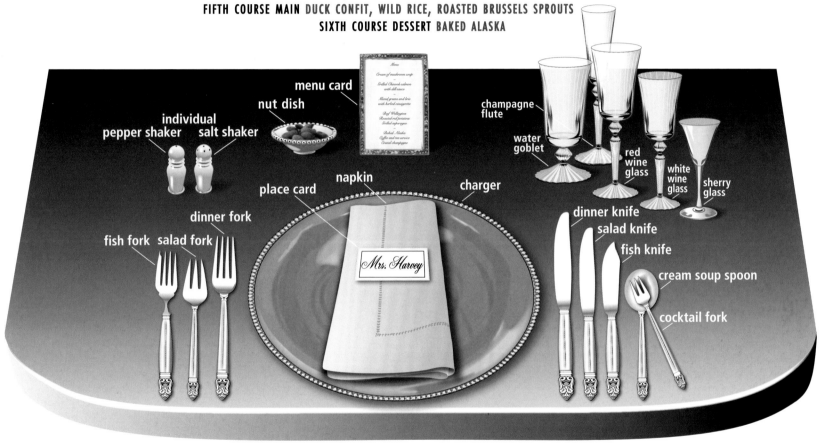

DINING TIPS

▸ Nuts may be eaten before the meal or in between courses.

▸ When several wines are served, it's acceptable not to finish each glass.

▸ Place two fingers on the rim of your glass to signal you don't want any more wine, saying quietly, "No, thank you."

▸ Break eye contact with other diners and look into your glass when drinking.

PREPARING THE TABLE

Dessert may be the highlight of your dinner party.

- Bring cups and saucers to the table with dessert. They are not pre-set as part of a dinner place setting.

- Prepare ahead of time a tray that holds cups and saucers with a sugar and creamer set, liqueur or cordial glasses, teaspoons and napkins for use preferably away from the dining table.

- Teaspoons and salad forks are good substitutes for dessert spoons and forks. Continental (European) dessert spoons are larger than teaspoons and dessert spoons, and they may be substituted with a place spoon.

Serving tips

- Place the point of a piece of pie or cake towards the diner.

- Serve coffee, tea, champagne, port or dessert wines during or after dessert.

- Move your guests away from the dining room table to another location for a winding down of the evening. Serve after dinner chocolates or mints, espresso, coffee, liqueurs or cordials after dessert.

DINING TIPS

▸ *The spoon above your dessert plate is used for dessert*, not for coffee. The teaspoon that is used for coffee or tea service is placed on top of the saucer along the right side of the cup; or placed to the right of the dessert plate at the time of the dessert service.

▸ After using the teaspoon, place it back on the saucer. Never lay it directly on the table after it has been used.

▸ In between bites, rest your dessert spoon on the underplate, not in the dessert dish or bowl.

▸ Avoid clanking your spoon against the sides of your dish, trying to get the last of the dessert.

The Dessert Course

"We must have pie. Stress cannot exist in the presence of pie."

~David Mamet

Option One
Place a spoon on the table at the beginning of the dessert course, after all previous course flatware has been removed.

Option Two
A dessert spoon with the handle facing to the right has been pre-set as part of the place setting before dinner begins.

Option Three (American style)
A dessert fork with the handle facing to the right has been pre-set as part of the place setting before dinner begins.

Option Four
Place a fork or spoon on the plate with the dessert and bring to the table for each dinner guest.

Option Five (Continental style)
Dessert fork with handle facing left and spoon with handle facing right have been pre-set as part of the place setting before dinner begins.

CONTINENTAL STYLE OF EATING DESSERT USING A FORK AND SPOON

Beginning to cut into dessert

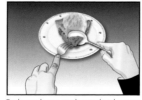

Fork used as a pusher to load spoon

Bringing dessert to your mouth

Begin with your dessert spoon in your right hand and the dessert fork, *tines down*, in your left hand. Tilt the spoon so that the side of your spoon becomes the cutting edge, press down and cut a bite of dessert. At the same time, use the dessert fork as a pusher to load the dessert spoon. *Eat from the dessert spoon*, not the fork. Continue holding the *fork in your left hand and the spoon in your right hand*, putting them down into a resting position only to take a drink, to pause, or to indicate you are finished eating.

The Cheese Course

"A meal without cheese is like a kiss without a squeeze."

~ Kathy's Grandpa Lee

A developing trend in America is serving a cheese course. The Europeans have been serving cheese to end a meal for centuries. It can be simple to elaborate.

Cheese is so versatile that you can serve it...

- with cocktails to begin a dinner party or gathering
- as an appetizer course to begin a sit-down meal
- on top of an individual salad when serving a salad course; or during a salad course, pass a platter of cheese around the table for guests to serve themselves
- after the main course as a separate course; either before or after dessert; or in place of dessert

TALKING CHEESE

Your best friend when serving cheese will be the local cheesemonger at your supermarket. This specialist will help you select the types of cheeses for your event along with breads or crackers, condiments and wines that pair well with your selection.

- Most cheese belongs to one of four basic categories: aged, soft, firm or blue.
- When serving several cheeses on a platter or board, provide a separate knife for cutting each cheese to prevent mixing the flavors.

| for hard cheese | for soft cheese | for semi-soft cheese | for semi-hard cheese | for serving cheese |

- For maximum flavor, allow cheese to rest from thirty minutes to two hours at room temperature before serving. Firm cheeses take longer to come to room temperature than soft cheeses, and the winter versus summer temperatures will alter the time requirements. Check with the store's cheesemonger for recommended serving temperatures.
- Offer bread or high quality crackers to cleanse the palate between bites of different types of cheese.
- Maintain original shape (wheel, cylinder, pyramid, slab) as much as possible when slicing individual servings of cheese. For example, the host may start by cutting a small pie shape wedge out of a wheel of Brie and the guests repeat the process.
- Remove rinds on firm cheeses. It is your personal preference whether to remove rind or not on soft cheese, such as triple crème.
- For fun, label each cheese with a cheese pick or place card.
- When storing cheese, remove the plastic wrap that the cheese comes in and refrigerate cheeses separately in breathable cheese paper or wax paper.

SERVING CHEESE

Cheese as an Hors d'Oeuvre

Preparing the hors d'oeuvre table

- Place cheese on a platter or cutting board with bread or crackers for serving before the meal in an area away from the dining table, such as a library table, coffee table, kitchen island, deck or patio.
- Provide a stack of salad or hors d'oeuvre plates, knives and forks or both if needed for each guest in the same area as the cheese platter.
- Provide small spoons and forks for serving dishes holding condiments such as olives and nuts. This eliminates the need for guests to use their fingers to serve themselves from communal serving dishes.

Cheese options

- Serve one large wheel of a single cheese for a dramatic impact.
- Arrange cheeses on the platter starting from mild to robust. Consider a selection of textures as well as flavors.
- Serve only cheeses from one region; serve the same type of cheese from several different regions; serve a mix of goat, sheep and cow's milk cheese.

Antipasto platter suggestion

Alongside the cheese serve sliced, cured meats such as:

~ Prosciutto or Soppresata (salami)

~ grilled or fresh vegetables

~ olives, nuts, dried or fresh fruit, or spreads

~ preserves, chutneys, or pesto

Cheese as an Appetizer Course

Preparing the table

- If the appetizer is the first course of the meal, pre-set appetizer on individual salad plates before guests are seated.
- Place individual knife, fork or both if needed at each place setting.

Cheese and condiment options

- Serve one to three types of cheese such as goat, brie, or blue cheese with condiments that are either cold or warm, like olives, roasted garlic, beets or sautéed mushrooms.
- Serve a mini-antipasto plate which contains your choice of cheese, cured meat, olives, grilled vegetables, or nuts.
- Bread or high-quality crackers may be placed on individual plates with the cheese or in a breadbasket and passed around the table.

A crowd pleaser

Serve baked goat cheese, olives and roasted garlic cloves in individual ramekins. Pre-set this hot appetizer on salad or accent plates minutes before guests are seated. Use a small knife to spread the cheese and place the condiments onto a slice of bread.

Cheese as part of a Salad Course

Preparing the table

- If the salad is the first course of the meal, pre-set salad on individual salad plates before guests are seated. Or, pre-set empty salad plates before guests are seated for guests to serve themselves from a communal serving bowl.
- Place individual fork, or fork and knife at each place setting.

Cheese options

- Serve crumbled, shaved, or shredded cheese mixed with the salad greens.
- Serve grated cheese from a small serving bowl with its own serving spoon. Pass around the table for individuals to serve themselves.
- Serve slices of cheese across the top of an individual salad.

Be creative with your salad

Purchase or make deep fried mozzarella sticks. Shave large curls of Parmesan cheese. Or, warm ¾″ thick rounds of goat cheese for a few seconds in the microwave and place beside, or on top of, an individual salad.

Cheese in place of Dessert

Preparing the table

- Pre-plate and serve cheese on individual salad or dessert plates for each dinner guest.
- Provide a knife and a salad or dessert fork, when necessary.

Cheese options

- Serve one to three types of cheese such as a goat, triple crème or fresh ricotta.
- Sweet condiments elevate cheese to a satisfying dessert. Consider serving

sweet chutneys, preserves or honey on top of the cheese or alongside the cheese in a small dish.

- Fruit condiments may be a cluster of grapes, dried or seasonal fresh fruits such as pears, figs, and stoned fruits. Avoid citrus fruits.
- Nut condiments may be roasted or caramelized nuts such as walnuts, pistachios, hazelnuts, pecans or almonds.

Add an impressive touch

Bread choices vary from plain or toasted baguettes to sweeter dessert breads such as thinly sliced, plain or toasted banana bread, or raisin nut bread. High-quality fruit and nut crackers are good options as well.

Cheese after the Dessert Course

Preparing the table
- Serve on individual dessert plates at the dining table.
- Provide a knife and a dessert fork when necessary.

Cheese options
- Serve one to three cheeses with bread or high-quality crackers.
- Serve cheese with dried or fresh fruit, and nuts on a communal platter or board at the dining table. Equip the platter with utensils to cut the cheese and place on individual plates.

A nice complement to cheese

Champagne, the little black dress of wine, or dessert wines are perfect beverages to serve with cheese. Finish with coffee or espresso.

How to eat cheese and olives

Soft cheese is cut from a wedge and placed on an individual plate, spread on a cracker or piece of bread and brought to the mouth with your fingers.

Firm cheese is sliced, transferred to an individual plate, and may be eaten with or without a cracker or piece of bread.

Olives may be eaten with your fingers in one bite if they are small, or in two bites if the olive is large.

Note to host: provide a small olive fork or spoon for guests to remove the olives from the bowl and transfer to their individual plates.

Entertainment made fun and easy

Cheese as the main attraction

- *We're not cooking tonight party:* The host asks each guest to bring their favorite cheese on a plate and a bottle of wine. Cheese knives, glassware, breads or crackers, nuts, cured meats and dessert are provided by the host.
- *Game night party:* Serve a variety of wine, champagne or both and an antipasto platter. Prepare a fun, interactive game for your guests to play, such as dominoes, marathon Monopoly, cell phone Charades, poker or Heads Up.
- *French theme party:* Host provides French wine or champagne and bread. Guests bring only types of French cheese.
- *Cheese fondue party:* Fondue is a crowd-pleaser, easy to make, and is a perfect way for the host to spend time with guests. Not all cheeses are right for making fondue, so be sure to find a good recipe. Suggestions for foods to dip: cubed French bread, cut fresh vegetables, apples and cooked or cured meat pieces.

Say "cheese" please – a slice of history

Although we don't know the specific origin of cheese making, we can surmise that it goes back 8,000-10,000 years to the domestication of milk-producing animals. Like many discoveries, cheese most likely came about by accident. Arabic legend holds that cheese was discovered by a merchant traveling across the Sahara, bringing along milk stored in a sheep stomach-lined pouch. As he traveled across the hot desert, the merchant found that his milk somehow magically transformed. The magic, it turns out, was the sun activating the rennin enzyme in the pouch which made the milk turn into curds and whey – the basic components of cheese.

Mastering Difficult-to-Eat Foods

When in doubt, follow the lead of the host.

Vegetables

Artichokes - Hold the base of the artichoke with one hand, take the outer leaves off one by one with your fingers. The edible part is at the base of the leaf where it is  attached to the heart. Dip the edible portion in a sauce, scrape off the bottom of the leaf by closing your teeth on it and pulling the leaf outward. Discard the leaves into a small bowl provided for each guest or onto the side of your plate. Continue until you get to the center of the artichoke (heart), pull off the center leaves for one last dip. Scoop out the choke (fuzzy part) that covers the artichoke heart and discard. Cut the heart with a knife and fork, and enjoy.

Asparagus - Pierce one or two asparagus spears at a time with your fork and cut spears into bite-sized pieces to eat. If the asparagus spear is cooked *al dente* (firm) and has no sauce on it, you may pick up a spear with your fingers to eat.

Cherry tomatoes - Pierce with a fork while holding a knife blade at the base of the tomato to steady it; slice in half and eat. If it is small, it may be eaten whole.

Corn on the cob - It is a matter of personal preference whether you eat the kernels *along the cob* or whether you eat in a *circular pattern* around the cob. The objective is to eat the corn neatly.

Green beans - Don't eat a long green bean whole. Pierce one to three beans with your fork, cut into *bite-sized pieces* with your knife and eat.

Seafood and escargot

Caviar - Remove a small spoonful of caviar from the bowl and place on a toast point, blini (small pancake), a plain cracker or on your plate. Eat plain or top with crème fraiche or other condiments.

Escargot - When an escargot tong is provided, use the tongs to secure the shell on your plate with one hand. Remove the snail with a small escargot fork using your other hand. If no tongs are available, hold the shell down on your plate with your forefinger and thumb, removing the snail with a small fork. You may pierce a small piece of bread with a fork and dip in the garlic butter sauce that was poured over the escargot.

Raw oysters, mussels and clams on the half shell - Top the flesh with condiments varying from freshly squeezed lemon juice, seafood cocktail sauce, champagne or vodka. Otherwise, eat plain. Secure the shell with one hand. Using your other hand, take a seafood fork to loosen the flesh from the shell, then put down your fork. If a fork is not provided, use your fingers to loosen the flesh. Tip the wide end of the shell into your mouth and let the flesh slide in whole.

Steamed clams and mussels - The shell opens during steaming. Don't eat an unopened clam or mussel – it is spoiled. Steady the opened shell between your forefinger and thumb, and then pull out the clam using a seafood fork or your fingers if a fork is not provided. Discard your shells in a bowl or on your plate. When all the clams have been eaten you may consume the remaining broth by using your spoon. Or, you may spear a small piece of bread with your fork to dip into the garlic butter sauce.

Whole fish - With the fish head pointed towards your right hand (opposite if you are left handed), insert your fish knife at the gill until you feel the fish's spine. Then slice under the flesh towards the tail. Using your fork and fish knife, lift the filet from the bone and place on your plate. Lift the exposed spine with your fingers and place in a separate bone dish or on your plate. This will free the second filet.

Miscellaneous foods

Bacon - If it is cooked limp, eat with a knife and fork; if it is crisp, pick up and eat with your fingers.

Cupcakes - Cupcakes piled high with frosting may be eaten with a fork and knife. Remove the cupcake wrapper and any fruit or fondant artwork on the top, cut the cupcake in half and lay the flat side down on the dessert plate. Cut into bite-sized pieces and eat with a fork. For smaller cupcakes (and no flatware is provided) remove the wrapper and enjoy one bite at a time.

Kabobs - Tip the skewer at an angle on your plate, slide the food items off with a fork one or two at a time until all items are on your plate. If the food is stuck to the skewer, lay the skewer onto your plate and cut foods off with a knife and fork. Place a used skewer on the right side of your plate.

A Buffet *is a meal where people serve themselves various dishes from a table or countertop. Buffets are extremely versatile. Elegant wedding receptions to casual Super Bowl parties, backyard barbecues, and family get-togethers are perfect events for a buffet.*

Types of Buffet Service

Standing Buffet: guests serve themselves primarily finger foods on small plates, mingling for a short time. Generally, table seating is not offered.

True Buffet: guests pick up their food, beverage and flatware from the buffet tables and find a place to sit. If using paper or plastic plates, be sure to purchase sturdy ones. If you have limited seating, offer only fork-friendly foods.

Seated Buffet: guests serve themselves from the buffet table, and then sit at a table pre-set with glasses, flatware, napkins, and salt and pepper shakers. With this type of buffet, you're not limited to fork-only food.

Buffet table set-up options:

Against the wall
— a single line of guests *moves* from the left to the right *along one side* of the table set with a variety of foods.

Center of the room
— a single line of guests *moves* in one direction from left to right *around the table* set with a variety of foods.

Double-sided
— two single lines of guests *move* in one direction on *each side of the table*. The same food items are placed on both sides of the table. This setup is suggested for groups of 40 or more.

Beverage Table - a separate area for serving beverages away from the main food table to enhance traffic flow. Pre-set with glassware, napkins and necessary flatware.

Dessert Table - a separate area for serving dessert. Pre-set with napkins, dessert plates, and necessary forks or spoons.

PREPARING THE TABLE

- Stack plates no more than 16 plates high at the *beginning of the line*.

- Place flatware and napkins at the *end of the line* because it's awkward for guests to carry them while they are serving themselves.

- Set foods in accordance with the progression of the meal. Place the *hot foods* toward the *end of the buffet table* so the food stays warm as long as possible on your guests' plate.

- Provide serving utensils alongside each dish, including small spoons for dips and sauces.

- Use place cards to label foods, such as "gluten-free," "contains nuts" or "contains shellfish."

- Vary heights of the serving dishes by draping sturdy boxes with fabric. These will serve as bases for serving dishes as well as to increase useable space and add a dramatic flair to the table.

- Heat the water in a chafing dish by lighting sterno 20 minutes before placing food in a chafing dish.

- Put food on the buffet table 10-15 minutes prior to the serving time.

Don't run short of food

"We were towards the end of the buffet line at a friend's summer event. By the time we reached the food, there were several empty platters. The problem was two-fold. The host had not provided enough food and the guests before us had over-loaded their plates. Unfortunately, the host didn't have back-up food. Or, if they did, there was no one to replenish the food. We were forced to leave the party early to get something to eat."
                                                              ~ Rosemarie

Note: When hosting a buffet, the adage "less is more" does not apply. Provide plenty of food. If there is food left over, you can freeze it or offer your guests the opportunity to take some home.

DINING TIPS

▸ Serve yourself modest portions.

▸ Do not eat from your plate until seated.

▸ Avoid holding a drink glass in your hand while going through the buffet line.

▸ Do not go back for seconds until everyone has been served.

▸ Do not double dip your vegetables or chips from the buffet table into the sauces or dressing.

The Buffet

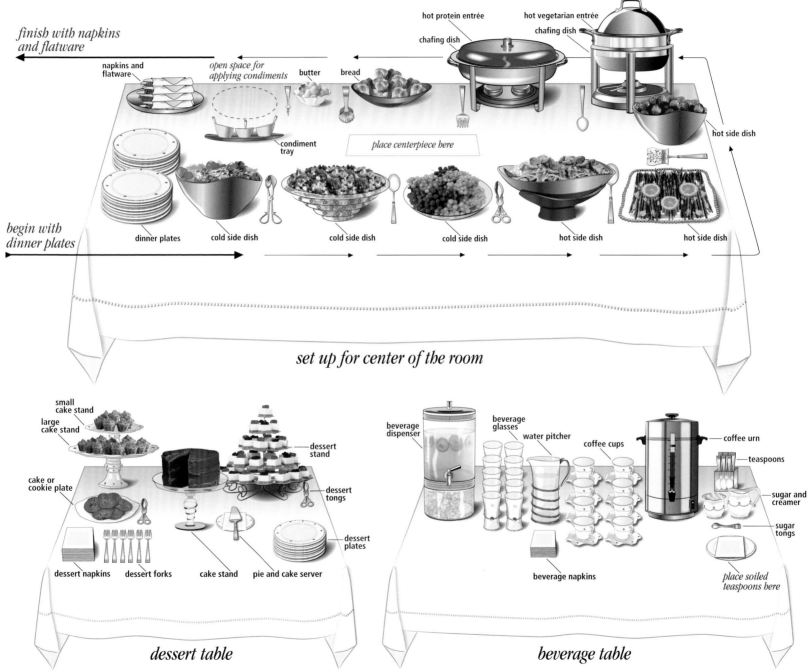

finish with napkins
and flatware

begin with
dinner plates

napkins and flatware

open space for applying condiments

condiment tray

butter

bread

place centerpiece here

dinner plates

cold side dish

cold side dish

cold side dish

hot side dish

hot side dish

hot protein entrée

hot vegetarian entrée

chafing dish

chafing dish

hot side dish

set up for center of the room

small cake stand

large cake stand

cake or cookie plate

dessert stand

dessert tongs

dessert plates

dessert napkins

dessert forks

cake stand

pie and cake server

dessert table

beverage dispenser

beverage glasses

water pitcher

coffee cups

coffee urn

teaspoons

sugar and creamer

sugar tongs

place soiled teaspoons here

beverage napkins

beverage table

Fondue *is French for "melt" or "blend;" fondue is a dish of melted cheese or chocolate served in a communal pot. It also refers to a method of cooking meat in hot oil or seasoned broth. Fondue is a perfect way for friends to gather around the warm glow of a flame.*

PREPARING THE TABLE AND FONDUE FOOD

- Provide each person with a salad, dinner or divided fondue plate, napkin, dinner fork and *two fondue forks* of the same color when using *oil or broth*, and *one fondue fork* when dipping into *cheese or chocolate*. When setting the table place fondue forks to the left of the dinner fork.

- Cheese and chocolate are best served in ceramic or earthenware fondue pots. Meats cooked in hot oil or broth are best served in stainless steel, copper, or cast iron pots using fondue fuel (denatured alcohol or Sterno). Electric fondue pots provide a steady heat source.

- Place no more than four fondue forks per hot oil or broth pot, since more people using the pot reduces the heat below the desired temperature. Too many forks get tangled and the food could drop to the bottom of the pot when being removed. *See Fun fondue penalties box.*

- Set individual or communal dipping bowls (ramekins) for each of the sauces or condiments.

- When serving cheese fondue, provide cubes of French bread which include a bit of the crust. This helps keep the bread on the fork after it is placed in the cheese. Pat dry cubes of meat for dipping into hot oil or seasoned broth.

Mini-sized fondue pots - a nice touch!

Serve cheese or chocolate fondue individually using mini-sized ceramic fondue pots.

Place the individual fondue pot on each dinner plate before guests are seated. Foods to be dipped may be placed on the individual's plates or on communal serving platters.

Cheese fondue may begin the meal as an appetizer. Chocolate fondue may conclude any dinner party.

Fun fondue penalties

Before your fondue event begins, announce the penalties. You're only limited by your imagination!

- If a participant drops a piece of food in the pot, they have to kiss the opposite sex to their left.

- If someone forgets to stir the pot, they have to properly stir their bread into the cheese and serve it to the person on their right.

- If someone puts their mouth on the fondue fork they have to sing a song.

- If successful in not getting caught when stealing another person's fork from the pot, the perpetrator announces they stole the food item. They get to ask a personal question of the victim. If you are the victim and catch the thief, you get to state the punishment.

DINING TIPS

▷ Pierce the food with a fondue fork and dip in the pot. Once cooked or dipped, let the excess oil, cheese or chocolate fall back into the pot. With your dinner fork, *slide the food from the fondue fork* onto your plate. Rest the fondue fork on your plate and *eat with a dinner fork.*

▷ Dip your bread deep into the cheese fondue pot and stir in a slow, zig-zag, figure-eight motion. This helps to blend the cheese.

▷ When cooking foods in oil or broth, have one fondue fork in the pot and the other one cooling on your plate.

▷ Do not double dip your food into communal fondue pots or sauces.

Dipping into the history of fondue

We find historical references to cooking and sharing a communal meal from one cooking pot dating back as far as 800 BC in Greece. During the middle ages in the French region of Burgundy, vineyard workers kept a single pot of hot oil in the fields where they cooked meat to eat and continued working.

In the 1700s, the Swiss styled the open fire communal cooking pot into a fondue, using aged cheese and bread to feed families during the cold winter months. In the 1950s - '70s Americans dipped crusted bread chunks on a skewer into a fondue pot, filled with a warmed mixture of cheese and wine while enjoying the pleasure of one another's company. Enjoying a warm, melty meal over an open fire is ageless.

One- to Four-Course Dipping into Fondue

"What we did in the '70s I mostly outgrew. With one big exception – making fondue!"

~ Pauletta

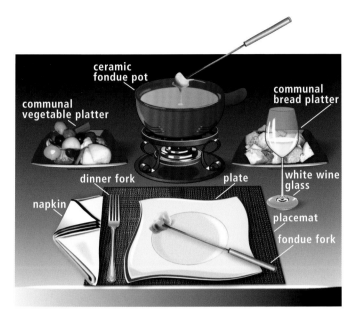

Communal cheese fondue

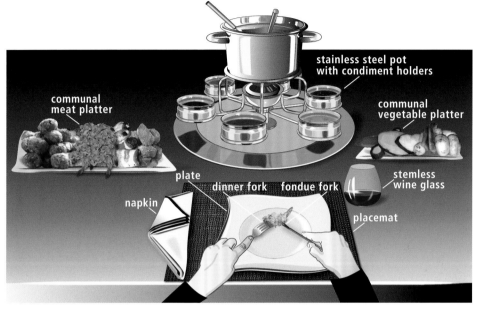

Communal oil or seasoned broth fondue

Communal chocolate fondue pot,
desserts and fruits individually pre-plated

Suggestions for Fondue Entertaining
- as part of an hors d'oeuvre-only party
- cheese fondue and wine or champagne party
- casual meal featuring an oil fondue as the main attraction
- chocolate fondue dessert-only with friends
- as any part of a progressive dinner stop
- serve cheese fondue away from the dining table and then bring your guests to the dining table for the main course of your choosing
- serve main course dinner at the dining table, and chocolate fondue in your living room

One- to Four-Course Options

One-course – choose one type of fondue – cheese, oil or broth, chocolate

Two-course – choose two types of fondue; or choose one fondue and a non-fondue course

Three-course – choose three types of fondue; or choose two fondues and one non-fondue course; or one fondue and two non-fondue courses

Four-course – choose three types of fondue and begin with a salad course; or intersperse any non-fondue course and any combination of cheese, oil or broth, or chocolate fondue course

Sushi Savvy

Sushi is a handmade Japanese finger food rolled with rice. Served American style, sushi is more of a "laid back" experience compared to sushi served traditionally in Japan. A sushi party may be as simple as purchasing the food at a market or restaurant, or as elaborate as making everything yourself.

Begin and end a sushi dinner event with an oshibori, a warm, wet towel used to clean fingers. They are passed on a tray, used and collected before the meal begins and repeated at the end of the meal.

Miso Soup

Miso: a hot broth made from fermented soybean and rice paste, often containing seaweed and tofu. Served at the beginning of the meal.

Common types of sushi

Nigiri: pieces of raw fish such as salmon or tuna served on top of rice and always served in pairs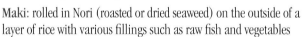

Maki: rolled in Nori (roasted or dried seaweed) on the outside of a layer of rice with various fillings such as raw fish and vegetables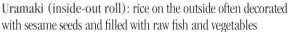

Uramaki (inside-out roll): rice on the outside often decorated with sesame seeds and filled with raw fish and vegetables

Sashimi: bite-sized pieces of raw, chilled fish, often served with rice on the side in a small rice bowl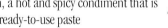

Condiments

Wasabi: Japanese horseradish, a hot and spicy condiment that is freshly grated, powdered or a ready-to-use paste

Soy sauce: made from boiled soybeans, this salty, brown sauce is mixed with wasabi in a small dish at the beginning of the meal

Ginger: thinly sliced, pickled ginger is used as a palate cleanser and eaten between bites or different types of sushi

How to hold chopsticks

Begin by resting the upper chopstick between the index finger and the middle finger, while steadying with the thumb.

Place the lower chopstick between the bottom of the thumb and the tip of the ring finger. Only the upper chopstick moves when you pick up the food.

Beverage and dessert options

Green tea: served warm in individual ceramic or porcelain tea cups

Sake, a fermented rice wine, may be served one of three ways:
- chilled - serve in a small glass, similar to a double-sized shot glass but made of thin, elegant glass
- warm - heat individual sake vessel in the microwave for 20-30 seconds and serve in sake cups
- at room temperature - serve in sake cups

Dessert: green tea ice cream, Japanese sweets

Don't be that guest...

- who eats your sushi or sashimi with a knife or fork.
- who slurps your miso soup.
- who sticks your chopsticks upright into a bowl of rice or into a piece of food, who licks your chopstick, or who waves or points them at someone.

DINING TIPS

▸ Pick up your miso soup bowl. Rest it in the palm of one hand and use your other hand to tilt the bowl to your mouth and drink. Use chopsticks to eat tofu or pieces of vegetables in the miso bowl.

▸ Use the *broad end of the chopsticks* to remove sushi from a *communal platter.* Most sushi may be eaten with your fingers or from the *pointed ends of the chopsticks.*

▸ Nigiri sushi is traditionally eaten with your fingers and dipped fish side down into the soy sauce.

▸ Sashimi is eaten only with chopsticks and dipped into the soy sauce.

▸ Place chopsticks in a chopstick rest with the pointed end facing left, if you are right-handed. If no chopstick rest is provided, place chopsticks together on the plate, not the tabletop.

▸ Lift the individual rice bowl upwards to your mouth while eating the rice with your chopsticks.

▸ Hold tea cup with one hand and rest it in the palm of the other hand, tipping it upward to your mouth to drink.

One- to Three-Course Sushi Affair

"Sushi parties take time and effort to prepare, but your guests are guaranteed to enjoy themselves which makes it all worthwhile."

~ Miki Sakata Pinguelo

Suggestions for entertaining with sushi

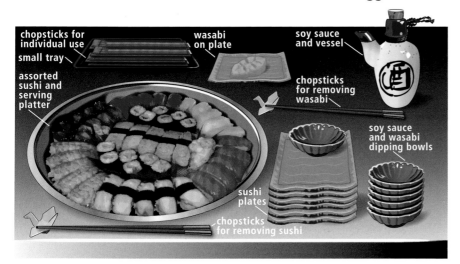

Guests serve themselves
- sushi only with tea, sake or champagne
- as part of a cocktail and hors d'oeuvre hour beginning a dinner party
- as part of an hors d'oeuvre-only party
- as part of a progressive dinner party

One- to Three-Course Options – served family style

One-course – assorted sushi served with side dishes such as rice, seaweed salad and edamame beans

Two-course – beginning with a miso soup course; second course assorted sushi served with a variety of side dishes

Three-course – beginning with miso soup; assorted sushi and side dishes; Japanese desserts

Two- to Three-Course Options

First course: starting with plated miso soup

Second course: sushi and side dishes are served family style from platters and bowls
Third course: green tea ice cream, *optional*

Entertaining with Themed Dinner Parties

"Variety is the soul of pleasure."
~ Apra Behn

Themed parties add excitement and create a memorable experience for your next dinner party. Guests enjoy the opportunity to take an active part in the party by dressing up or bringing a themed item. Table settings, props, food, beverage choices and activities all contribute to making your themed party a success.

Hors d'oeuvre party

Why not have an adventurous hors d'oeuvre party? Presentation is everything! Try serving hor d'oeuvres on tasting spoons, mini-plates and bowls, bamboo picks or artistically arranged platters. Be creative with garnishes by using edible flowers, banana leaves or herbs. Provide finger foods only, plates and napkins. Keep it simple and serve a signature cocktail. Dessert is optional. Add a bubble machine and let the party begin!

Options:
- Host provides all hors d'oeuvres and beverages.
- Host provides hors d'oeuvres, guests bring wine or champagne.
- Host provides beverages, guests bring hors d'oeuvres with a recipe card.

Progressive dinner

A progressive dinner is a casual and fun dinner party that moves or "progresses" from one home to the next, not to exceed four stops. Each host is responsible for their assigned food course. An advantage to a progressive dinner party is the workload and cost is divided among hosts, and the stress of a multi-course dinner is reduced. The dinner menu may be three to four courses and some courses such as the main course may take longer than an hors d'oeuvre course. Parties may be designed with theme-related foods and decorations. Ideally, it is nice if the homes are within walking distance. Parties may even begin and end at the same house. If guests are carpooling, this allows them to pick up their car where the party began.

Menu course options:
- Cocktails and hors d'oeuvres
- Salad, soup or pasta
- Main course
- Dessert and after-dinner drinks

Consider having a cheese course, fondue or sushi at any one of the stops.

Tips for a successful party:
- Invite six to 12 people or more.
- Plan foods that can be prepared in advance.
- Allow 45 to 90 minutes at each stop, depending on the course.

Sushi party
Ways to make your sushi party memorable:

Wouldn't it be wonderful to hire your own sushi chef to prepare the food in front of your guests? Or, begin with an origami making session? What about having a chopstick competition to see who can pick up the most popcorn pieces in one minute? Make it the best out of three timing sessions so that guests become efficient using chopsticks. See pages 54 and 55 for table setting and dining instructions.

Setting up the theme:
- Create a Japanese playlist of music to have playing as guests arrive.
- Hang Japanese paper lanterns around eating area or hang at the front door.
- Fill a basket at the front door with disposable booties for guests to change into upon their arrival.
- Set up low tables, such as coffee tables. Use tatami (straw) mats or Japanese pillows on the floor for each guest to sit on while dining.
- Decorate with flowers such as orchids, chrysanthemums, azaleas, cherry blossoms, lotus or a bonsai plant.

A nice touch
- Offer each lady a flower for her hair as she arrives.
- Use a combination of decorative chopsticks and rests, Japanese teacups and Japanese fans as table favors
- Hire a masseuse to give 10-minute shoulder rubs for each guest.
- Host, servers and masseuse dress in Japanese apparel.

Dickens "A Christmas Carol" evening

Christmas with Dickens is the condensed book version of Charles Dickens classic holiday novel, *A Christmas Carol*, and can be read to an audience in 30 minutes. The story is told in five staves (excerpts).

Use this story as entertainment for a five or six course dinner. See pages 39 and 41. Assign guests staves to read, or one talented reader may read the entire story. Staves range from three to 10 minutes long and can be read between courses. If you don't want to serve a multi-course dinner, consider reading the story during the hors d'oeuvre hour or following dinner in the living room with after-dinner drinks and desserts. For an extra touch, the readers and guests can dress in period costumes. Sound effects are a simple and wonderful contribution to the story. For example, when Scrooge is frightened in the first stave by Marley's Ghost, put a chain in a metal bucket or container and drag the chains across the metal to simulate the chains and cashboxes that weighed down Scrooge's deceased business partner. Do this out of sight, and then drop the bucket at the appropriate time...you'll have your guests on the edge of their seats!

A fog machine is fun too, as well as someone playing a flute, harmonica, violin or a piano in a later stave when the Cratchits are enjoying their holiday meal.

'70s party
Nothing was too outrageous for the '70s.

Big hair, music from the Bee Gees, Donna Summer and Sonny & Cher, fluorescent floral-print fabrics, bell-bottoms, disco balls, the hippie movement, toga parties and a desire for peace all signified the '70s. This party almost demands it be a costume disco party.

Greet your guests at the door and hand them a card containing a word or phrase to use throughout the night. Get in the groove and try some of these: *hey man, groovy, peace, can you dig it?, ya know, you are the man* or *the man, far-out, totally, get down-get funky, chill, cool, to the max, dream on, back-at-cha, that's sick, catch you on the flip side, fab, boogy down, right on!*

Consider asking someone ahead of time to demonstrate some of the '70s dance moves such as the hustle, funky chicken, YMCA, the jerk, the bump and disco pair dancing.

Party favors: headbands, love beads, yo-yos, pet rocks or tie-dyed anything. Arrange these as a centerpiece or at each individual place setting.

This is a perfect party for a potluck buffet. Have everyone bring a dish from the '70s. Or, the hostess can prepare all the food featuring casseroles, sandwiches with alfalfa sprouts, deviled eggs, peanut butter in celery, popcorn from a popcorn popper, granola, ambrosia salad, Jello salad in a mold, potato chips with onion or clam dip, fondue and Spam. You can even serve brownies with a card reading "contains nuts but no weed." See pages 50 and 51 for Buffet setup.

Dessert buffet

Feature a dessert buffet for a holiday open house, a bridal shower or a birthday party. Serve a variety of desserts in creative containers such as individual tasting spoons, mini-bowls or plates.

Satisfy all chocolate lovers with a fondue. Place one to three fondue pots on your buffet table. Feature choices of milk, dark or white chocolate for guests to dip cubes of angel food or pound cake, cookies or biscotti and assorted fruits such as strawberries, bananas or pineapples. See page 53 for Dipping into Fondue.

Add a build-your-own ice cream parfait station with toppings, fruit, nuts, whipped cream and sauces.

Provide beverages, napkins and dessert plates with the necessary flatware.

Party on!
More theme party ideas with table setting references:

Seafood Party: serve Spanish Paella, hire a Flamenco instructor; page 31, Three-Course Dinner

Soulfood Party: serve chicken and waffle brunch; page 25, Weekend Brunch

Oscar Night Party: featuring beef tenderloin; page 35, Four-Course Fabulous Affair

Casino Night: serve assorted cold and hot foods; page 51, The Buffet

Ugly Sweater Party: ruin that ugly sweater with spaghetti with turkey meatballs and marinara sauce; page 27, One-Course Dinner

Murder Mystery Party: invite guests to dress in their character's costume, conclude with bread pudding and chocolate chunks; page 39, Five-Course Sophisticated Affair

Tea and Coffee Cup Etiquette

- Stir your tea or coffee gently using a teaspoon. Avoid clanking it against the sides of the cup.

- When sitting at a table, raise the cup to drink, leaving the saucer on the table. When sitting on a sofa, with a low table in front of you, lift the cup and saucer together.

Correct way of holding coffee or tea cup. No extended pinkie finger.

Correct coffee or tea cup holding when standing or sitting away from table.

Correct placement of teaspoon. Once used, place it back on the saucer, not the tabletop.

Incorrect placement of resting teaspoon

How to Hold Stemware

Hold white wine or champagne glass by the stem so it remains chilled longer and does not alter the aroma or flavor. Hold a red wine glass by the base of the bowl, using two fingers and a thumb.

Correct champagne glass holding

Correct white wine glass holding

Correct red wine glass holding

Incorrect holding of all stemware

Styles of Dining including Silent Signals

AMERICAN STYLE

1. Starting position

2. Demonstrating placement of handles in hands with fork tines up

3. Turn flatware over, pierce food item with fork tines down, cutting one bite at a time with knife.

4. Place knife on right side of the plate, shift fork from left to right hand, turning fork tines up before transferring food to your mouth.

5. "I'm resting," when pausing between bites with fork tines up

6. "I'm finished," with fork tines up

CONTINENTAL (EUROPEAN) STYLE

Used worldwide, this is a quieter and more refined method of eating.

1. Starting position

2. Demonstrating placement of handles in hands with fork tines up

3. Turn flatware over, pierce food item with fork tines down, cutting one bite at a time with knife.

4. Knife remains in right hand pointed down towards the plate, fork remains in left hand with tines down throughout meal. Transfer food to your mouth with fork tines down.

5. "I'm resting," when pausing between bites with fork tines down

6. "I'm finished," with fork tines down

Don't end up in the dining hall of shame

Caveman Style   Semi-Caveman Style   Oars in the water

RIGHT VS. LEFT
History of American and Continental Eating Styles

Americans and Europeans both held their forks in their right hand to dine until the mid-1800s. Eating styles changed in Europe when the upper classes in England and France made a shift – which was to "not shift." Instead, they kept their forks in their left hands. The new style was not only seen as more graceful and elegant, but also as a way of distinguishing the upper class from the rest. However, that sophisticated division didn't last long. Soon all French and English classes adopted this style. However, for whatever reason, Americans did not adopt the Continental style, and continue to use the American "zig-zag" style of transferring the fork from the left hand to the right.

Due to globalization, we see a growing trend in America toward the Continental style. It's easier and, like in the 1800s, is considered a more polished method of eating.

Serving Utensils

Serving Forks

- pasta server 10-12"
- large serving 8-11"
- cold meat 7½"
- lemon, olive or pickle 4-6"

Serving Spoons

- buffet or stuffing 10-12"
- plain or pierced serving 10"
- berry 9½"
- tablespoon (plain) 8¾"
- tablespoon (pierced) 8¾"
- olive 7"
- jelly 6½"
- bon bon 6½"
- sugar 6¼"
- mustard 6"
- horse-radish 6"
- sugar tongs 4½"
- caviar, mother of pearl 4"
- lasagna or flat all-purpose server 11-13"

Miscellaneous Servers

- asparagus server 9-10"
- tomato or flat server 8"
- butter server 7"
- butter pick 5"

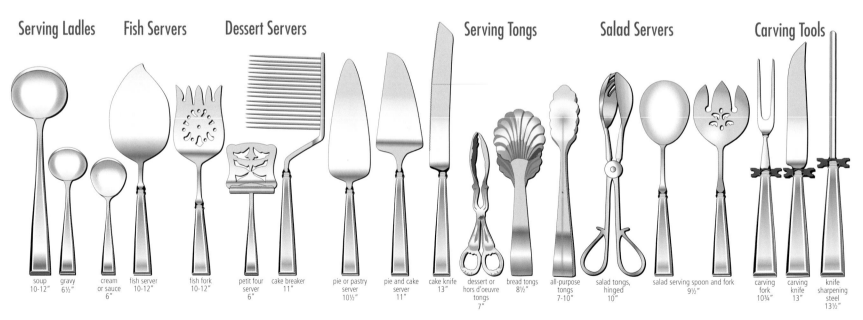

Serving Ladles

- soup 10-12"
- gravy 6½"
- cream or sauce 6"

Fish Servers

- fish server 10-12"
- fish fork 10-12"

Dessert Servers

- petit four server 6"
- cake breaker 11"
- pie or pastry server 10½"
- pie and cake server 11"
- cake knife 13"

Serving Tongs

- dessert or hors d'oeuvre tongs 7"
- bread tongs 8½"
- all-purpose tongs 7-10"
- salad tongs, hinged 10"

Salad Servers

- salad serving spoon and fork 9½"

Carving Tools

- carving fork 10¾"
- carving knife 13"
- knife sharpening steel 13½"

Each utensil serves a specific purpose, though many can perform multiple tasks. Measurements are estimates and not exact as sizes and shapes vary by manufacturer and date of production.

Flatware

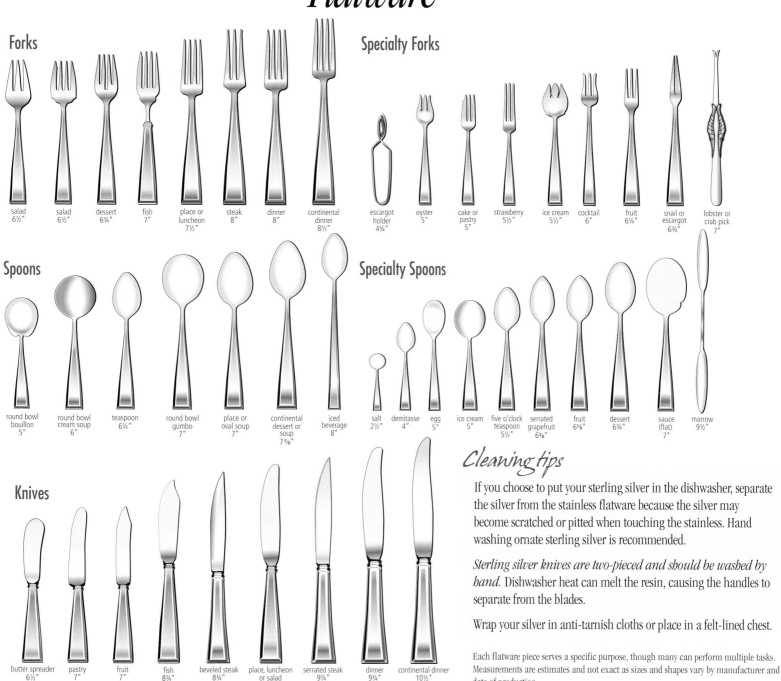

Forks

| salad 6½" | salad 6½" | dessert 6¾" | fish 7" | place or luncheon 7½" | steak 8" | dinner 8" | continental dinner 8½" |

Specialty Forks

| escargot holder 4¾" | oyster 5" | cake or pastry 5" | strawberry 5½" | ice cream 5½" | cocktail 6" | fruit 6¼" | snail or escargot 6¾" | lobster or crab pick 7" |

Spoons

| round bowl bouillon 5" | round bowl cream soup 6" | teaspoon 6¼" | round bowl gumbo 7" | place or oval soup 7" | continental dessert or soup 7⅝" | iced beverage 8" |

Specialty Spoons

| salt 2½" | demitasse 4" | egg 5" | ice cream 5" | five o'clock teaspoon 5½" | serrated grapefruit 6⅛" | fruit 6⅛" | dessert 6¾" | sauce (flat) 7" | marrow 9½" |

Knives

| butter spreader 6½" | pastry 7" | fruit 7" | fish 8¾" | beveled steak 8¾" | place, luncheon or salad 9" | serrated steak 9¼" | dinner 9¾" | continental dinner 10½" |

Cleaning tips

If you choose to put your sterling silver in the dishwasher, separate the silver from the stainless flatware because the silver may become scratched or pitted when touching the stainless. Hand washing ornate sterling silver is recommended.

Sterling silver knives are two-pieced and should be washed by hand. Dishwasher heat can melt the resin, causing the handles to separate from the blades.

Wrap your silver in anti-tarnish cloths or place in a felt-lined chest.

Each flatware piece serves a specific purpose, though many can perform multiple tasks. Measurements are estimates and not exact as sizes and shapes vary by manufacturer and date of production.

Serveware

Platters and Bowls

oval platters

soup tureen with ladle

large compote (fruit)

salad bowl

pasta bowl with stand

large serving bowl

rice bowl

Bowls and Tabletop Accessories

covered serving bowl

open vegetable bowl

gravy or sauce boat and underplate

salt and pepper shaker set

covered butter dish

jam pot with spoon

horseradish or mustard pot with spoon

caviar bowl with liner for ice

champagne bottle coaster

wine bottle coaster

Tabletop Accessories   Decanter and Pitchers

cake stand with or without dome

trifle bowl

cake plate

sandwich or dessert tray

condiment tray

bread basket

wine decanter

large or medium beverage pitcher

small beverage pitcher

small pitcher (for syrup or sauce)

Coffee and Tea Service

coffee server with sugar and creamer

latte mug

coffee mug

cappuccino cup and saucer

coffee cup and saucer

demitasse (espresso) cup and saucer

teapot

coffee server or teapot warmer

covered tea cup and saucer

tea cup and saucer

Sizes and shapes vary by manufacturer and date of production.

Dinnerware
for individual place settings

Plates

charger or service plate
12"

place plate
10½"

dinner plate
10½"

luncheon or accent plate
9"

crescent plate
(salad or bone)
9"

salad or dessert plate
8"

Plates

dessert plate
6-7"

bread and butter plate
6¼"

saucer
5¾"

appetizer plate
4-5"

Bowls

lidded soup bowl

soup or cereal bowl

soup or salad bowl

flat-rimmed soup plate

cream soup bowl

Bowls

lidded bouillon
cup and saucer

bouillon cup

pasta bowl

fruit saucer
or berry bowl

rice bowl

finger bowl

Specialty Accessories

artichoke plate

fondue plate

escargot plate

tasting spoon

Specialty Accessories

french fry
basket

shrimp cocktail
server
(two-piece with
ice liner)

seafood cocktail
glass

egg cup

syrup pitcher

individual salt
and
pepper shakers

salt cellar
and spoon

butter or
cocktail
sauce cup

nut dish

butter pat

dipping dish

Dessert

soda glass

parfait or
sundae glass

dessert dish

sherbet dish

Sizes and shapes vary by manufacturer and date of production.

Wine Service Tips

- Before guests arrive, remove any fingerprints or water spots on the glassware by using a lint-free cloth. Dampen one end and wipe the glass clean with the dry end, or use a dry microfiber cloth.

- Place a bottle of white, rosé, champagne or sparkling wine in an ice bucket filled with ice and water. Bottles will chill in approximately 20 minutes.

- Use wine charms or paper identification tags to identify each guest's glass when serving wine away from the table.

- Consider using universal wine glasses to serve either red or white wine. However, do not pour a red wine into the same glass that previously held white wine or vice versa in order not to mix the flavors.

Wine pouring finesse

~ Pour wine with the label facing the diner and turn the bottle slightly when finishing the pour to prevent drips.

~ Leave the wine glass on the table when pouring wine into a glass.

~ When pouring wine, hold the wine bottle no higher than an inch above the glass to prevent the wine from splashing out of the glass.

~ Pour no more than four ounces of wine in a glass or more than halfway full. This allows space for swirling the wine to enjoy the aroma and enhance the experience.

Don't be that guest...

who brings your pre-dinner glass of wine, cocktail or other beverage to the table where dinner will be served unless invited to do so by the host.

Glassware

Wine and Beverage

water goblet · iced beverage · red wine · white wine · hock (german riesling) · sherry

Specialty Wine

bordeaux grand cru (cabernet sauvignon, merlot) · pinot noir · burgundy grand cru (pinot noir) · zinfandel (chianti classico) · riesling grand cru · chablis (chardonnay) · montrachet (chardonnay) · sauterne (dessert) · rosé · stemless cabernet or merlot · stemless pinot noir · stemless riesling or sauvignon blanc

Champagne

toasting flute · hollow stem flute · trumpet flute · flute · tulip flute · saucer or coupe

Before Dinner Cocktail Glasses

zombie or chimney · collins · highball · double old fashioned · old fashioned or rocks · dizzy cocktail · mint julep cup · double shot · single shot · hurricane · poco grande · cocktail glass (martini) · coupette (margarita) · single malt whiskey

After Dinner Glasses

tequila · grappa · cognac · port · port sipper · brandy snifter and warmer · large brandy · irish coffee · irish coffee mug · liqueur or cordial

Beer

pilsner (tumbler) · pilsner (stemmed) · beer mug

Everyday Beverage Glasses

pint (tumbler) · cooler (tumbler) · beverage (tumbler) · juice (tumbler)

Sizes and shapes vary by manufacturer and date of production.

Setting up the Home Bar

The home bar is a designated area to serve both alcoholic and non-alcoholic beverages.

Liquors or spirits are alcoholic beverages distilled from grains, vegetables or fruits.

Liqueurs are alcohol based and made from nuts, seeds, herbs and spices.

Cordials are sweetened alcohols made from fruit.

The terms liqueurs and cordials are often used interchangeably.

Start with five basic liquors

- Gin
- Rum (Silver, Gold or Dark)
- Tequila
- Vodka
- Whiskey (Bourbon, Scotch or Rye)

Five suggested liqueurs or cordials

- Bailey's Irish Cream
- Contreaux
- Grand Marnier
- Kahlua
- Triple Sec

Your bar menu may be a simple "one-specialty drink," such as a lemon drop martini, whiskey sour, mojito, Manhattan or margarita.

Common mixers (non-alcoholic liquids added to cocktails) are orange or cranberry juice, tonic water or seltzer, cola or lemon-lime soda.

Simple syrup is used to sweeten cocktails. Make your own simple syrup of equal parts sugar and water, warm to a simmer and then chill before serving.

Bitters (a concentrated distillation of liquor and herbs, bark, roots and spices) are added in drops to a drink.

Wine choices: white wines, such as a Pinot Gris or Chardonnay; red wines, such as Pinot Noir or Cabernet Sauvignon; and possibly sparkling wines or champagne

Beer choices: offer one or two mainstream beers or lagers of medium strength or a selection of microbrew beers

Non-alcoholic choices: sparkling cider, flavored and plain bottled water, juices, soft drinks, non-alcoholic beer and wine

Garnishes for cocktails: lemon twists, lime wedges, maraschino cherries, fresh mint, celery, olives and cocktail onions; use assorted fresh fruits for added color in plain or exotic drinks

Other bar musts: a cocktail napkin for each drink, cocktail picks for martini olives and onions, straws and swizzle sticks; and don't forget to stock up on ice!

Stay on trend and purchase an updated cocktail recipe book to become a confident bartender (mixologist)

Hire a bartender or ask a friend to serve your guests if your group is larger than 10

Champagne and a spooky Halloween tour

"For Halloween I enjoy decorating the house with monsters and zombies that move and are surrounded by ample amounts of fog. I greet my guests with a glass of bubbly outside on the front steps where I have chilled champagne in a multi-bottle ice bucket and glasses set up on a table. Guests are escorted in small groups and given a tour of my haunted house. Hidden terrors are lurking around every corner."

~ Rosemarie

Porch bar

"I have limited space inside the house to set up a home bar during a dinner party. However, I have a large front porch where I can set up ice buckets, a punchbowl, and plenty of wine glasses. To keep it simple, I often have only bar glasses and feature one signature cocktail for guests to serve themselves upon their arrival."

~ Linda

Barware Accessories

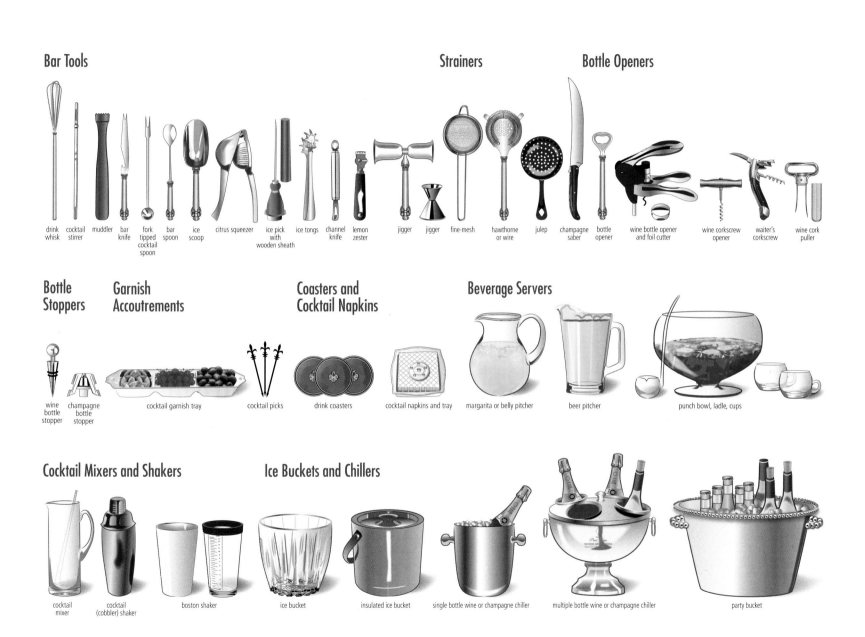

Bar Tools

drink whisk · cocktail stirrer · muddler · bar knife · fork tipped cocktail spoon · bar spoon · ice scoop · citrus squeezer · ice pick with wooden sheath · ice tongs · channel knife · lemon zester

Strainers

jigger · jigger · fine-mesh · hawthorne or wire · julep

Bottle Openers

champagne saber · bottle opener · wine bottle opener and foil cutter · wine corkscrew opener · waiter's corkscrew · wine cork puller

Bottle Stoppers

wine bottle stopper · champagne bottle stopper

Garnish Accoutrements

cocktail garnish tray · cocktail picks

Coasters and Cocktail Napkins

drink coasters · cocktail napkins and tray

Beverage Servers

margarita or belly pitcher · beer pitcher · punch bowl, ladle, cups

Cocktail Mixers and Shakers

cocktail mixer · cocktail (cobbler) shaker · boston shaker

Ice Buckets and Chillers

ice bucket · insulated ice bucket · single bottle wine or champagne chiller · multiple bottle wine or champagne chiller · party bucket

Sizes and shapes vary by manufacturer and date of production.

Check-off List and Timeline

"He who fails to plan is planning to fail"

~ Winston Churchill

DINNER PARTY PRE-PLANNING

Two to three weeks ahead

- ☐ Invite guests, asking for dietary needs such as food allergies to seafood, gluten, dairy or nuts.
- ☐ Order rental equipment (chairs, tables, serving dishes, beverage and wine glasses, dinnerware, flatware, tablecloths and cloth napkins, or any other equipment needs).
- ☐ Purchase party supplies (decorations, elegant paper napkins, candles, table favors, or any other needs).
- ☐ Enlist the help of a friend to assist you in serving, or perhaps hire a teenager to help with prep, serving and cleanup.
- ☐ Select or create music playlist.

One week before the party

- ☐ Create menu.
- ☐ Make grocery shopping list, including recipe ingredients and beverages.
- ☐ Purchase liquor, wine, mixers.

Two to three days before the party

- ☐ Perform household cleaning tasks inside and outside of the house.
- ☐ Complete set up tasks: iron tablecloths and napkins, set up extra chairs and tables if necessary, make place cards and menu cards.
- ☐ Set the table(s) one day to one week prior to dinner party.
- ☐ Shop for groceries, remembering food and drink garnishes.

Day before or day of the party

- ☐ Purchase flowers and plenty of ice.
- ☐ Set out serving dishes with serving utensils; label bowls and platters to indicate which foods go into which bowl or platter.
- ☐ Assemble hors d'oeuvres or side dishes that can be made ahead of time.

DINNER PARTY TIMELINE

Morning of the party

- Set up bar area for cocktail hour (ice bucket, beverage dispenser, punchbowl, mixers, glasses, napkins).
- Set out small plates, napkins, glassware, flatware (if any) for hors d'oeuvres.
- Set out dessert plates, serving pieces and dessert flatware in working area.
- Set out coffee server, cups and saucers, sugar and creamer set on a tray in service area for the dessert course. Set up coffee maker with coffee and water (to be turned on when ready to serve dinner).

Noon

- Assemble salad, cut up garnishes; keep chilled in refrigerator.
- Make sauces or salad dressings.
- Touch up floors, empty trash cans, double-check table settings.

Plan, plan, plan...

Allow ample time to cook your meal and to do last-minute tasks.

Two hours before guests arrive

- Ice the wine, beer, non-alcoholic beverages and mixers; set out bar condiments.
- Finalize making or baking hors d'oeuvres.
- Get dressed for the party.

Fifteen minutes before guests arrive

- Light the candles, start the fire in the fireplace, turn on the music.
- Set out hors d'oeuvres.

When guests arrive

- Greet guests at the door, take their coats and handbags, direct them to the hors d'oeuvres and beverages, and introduce them to other guests.

Ten minutes before serving dinner

- Turn on coffee pot for coffee with dessert.
- Pour chilled water into water glasses.
- Announce that dinner is ready to be served in ten minutes.

Manners Simply Put...

*"**Never** put a foil-covered plastic tray full of hors d'oeuvres in a hot oven.
Always enjoy the laughs and the camaraderie that comes with cleaning it up."*

~ Jon-Paul Genet

Always

- *Always* respond to an invitation within a week.

- *Always* arrive on time; no more than 15 minutes late and never early!

- *Always* take a hostess gift when attending a dinner party. A bouquet of flowers should be given in a vase. Attach a gift tag to all gifts, including wine.

- *Always* set forks on the left of the place setting and knives on the right with the blade facing the plate.

- *Always* place a napkin or coaster underneath your cocktail or wine glass before setting the glass on a coffee or cocktail table.

- *Always* use the beverage glasses on your right and the bread and butter plate on the left of your place setting.

- *Always* pass foods in one direction, moving to the right.

- *Always* pass salt and pepper shakers together – they are married!

- *Always* spoon away from yourself when eating soup.

- *Always* wait until guests have gone home before washing dishes, unless you've arranged for outside help or it's getting late and a few stragglers remain.

- *Always* find the host before departing to thank him or her for being included.

- *Always* send a thank you note to the host within a day or two of the dinner party. A handwritten thank you is still the most impressive.

Never

- *Never* show up at a dinner party with an uninvited friend or date and assume it's okay to bring children or pets.

- *Never* ask for a guided tour of the host's home.

- *Never* bring your cocktail hour glass to the dining table, unless instructed by your host.

- *Never* rearrange your assigned place card seating to suit yourself.

- *Never* dive in and start to serve yourself. Follow the lead of the host and don't begin to eat before he or she does, unless permission is given.

- *Never* eat like a caveman.

- *Never* push your plate away from you when finished with your course.

- *Never* be tempted to eat from your neighbor's plate.

- *Never* monopolize the conversation at a dinner party; avoid talking about controversial topics.

- *Never* acknowledge another guest's dining mistakes – that is a mistake itself, and there really isn't an etiquette police.

- *Never* perform personal grooming at the table such as applying lipstick or blowing your nose (especially into your napkin).

- *Never* get up from the dinner table and start removing dishes if the host declines your offer to help.

Always use a new piece of flatware for each course, starting from the outside and working inward toward the plate.

So now you know the answer to
Which Fork Do I Use?

Source Guide

Front cover
glassware, flatware, napkin ring - Juliska; napkin - Kim Seyburt

Page 10
blue plate, flatware, napkin, napkin ring - Juliska; place plate - Flora Danica by Royal Copenhagen

Page 11
soup plate, cup and saucer - Juliska

Page 12
plates, flatware - Juliska; coasters - Waterford

Page 13
champagne glass - Baccarat; bread basket - American Metalcraft

Page 14
plate - Juliska; champagne bucket - graphically created

Page 15
wine glass - Reidel; soup tureen - Lennox; clear glass plate and dessert dish - Royal Bavarian Crystal

Page 16
plate, flatware - Juliska; small spoon, sorbet glass and glass plate - Libbey

Page 19
charger, napkin ring - Juliska; napkin - Kim Seybert

Page 21
dinnerware, glassware, flatware, napkin - Juliska

Page 23
dinnerware, glassware, flatware, napkin and napkin ring - Juliska

Page 24
jam jar - Juliska

Page 25
dinnerware, glassware, flatware - Juliska; napkin ring - Michael Wainright; charger, fruit spoon - graphically created

Page 27
bread basket - American Metalcraft; dinnerware, glassware, flatware - Juliska; salad bowl - Nambé; napkin and napkin ring - unknown

Page 28
mug - Juliska; knife - J.A. Henckels, Int'l.; cutting board - unknown

Page 29
dinnerware, glassware, flatware - Juliska; napkin - graphically created; place mat - Chilewich

Page 30
cradle pasta bowl - Nambé

Page 31
dinnerware, glassware, flatware - Juliska; place mats - Chilewich; napkin - graphically created; napkin ring - Kim Seybert

Page 33
dinnerware, flatware - Juliska; glassware - Simon Pearce; slate and napkin - graphically created; tasting spoons - unknown

Page 35
charger, dinnerware, glassware, flatware, napkin ring - Juliska; napkin - Kim Seybert; salt and pepper shakers - unknown

Page 37
flatware - International Silver; glassware - Baccarat; napkin - Jan de Luz; charger, place card holder, salt and pepper shakers - unknown

Page 39
dinnerware - Villeroy & Boch; glassware - Baccarat; flatware - International Silver; charger - graphically created; cocktail dish with ice liner, salt cellar - unknown

Page 41
charger - Arte Italica; glassware - Baccarat; flatware - International Silver; napkin - Jan de Luz; nut dish and menu card holder - graphically created; salt and pepper shakers - unknown

Page 43
glassware - Waterford; flatware - International Silver; place card holder, charger and napkin - graphically created; salt cellar, pepper shaker - unknown

Page 45
dinnerware, glassware, flatware - Juliska; dessert dish - Royal Bavarian Crystal; glass plate - unknown

Page 46
cheese pick - Juliska; cheese knives - graphically created

Page 47
dinnerware, flatware, ramikan, butter spreader, salad plate - Juliska; small fork and spoon - Libbey; cheese knife - graphically created

Page 48
dinnerware, serveware - Juliska; glassware - Waterford; small spoons - Libbey; serving platter - graphically created

Page 49
artichoke plate - Bon Chef; escargot plate - unknown

Page 51
dinnerware, sugar and creamer - Juliska; serving bowl, pasta bowl - Nambé; dessert stand - Wilton; beverage dispenser - Arthur Court; coffeemaker - Coffee Pro; cake stands - Juliska; serving utensils, cake plate, sugar tong,

three bowls and one serving tray, forks and teaspoons - graphically created

Page 52
fondue forks - Tramontia

Page 53
dinnerware - Villeroy & Boch; wine glasses - Reidel; champagne flute - Waterford; flatware - Juliska; stainless steel pot and condiment holders, fondue forks - Tramontia; place mats - Chilewich; napkin and serving platters - graphically created; divided fondue plate and two fondue pots - unknown

Page 54
tray, chopsticks, rice bowl, miso soup bowl, sake glass, small tray - unknown

Page 55
serving platter - graphically created; small bowl - Pier 1; remainder unknown

Page 56
punchbowl - Libbey; tasting spoon - unknown

Page 57
charger - Arte Italica; dinnerware and serveware - Juliska; napkin - Jan de Luz; flatware and tray - graphically created

Page 58
teacup - Lomonosov; champagne glass - Waterford; wine glasses - Reidel; flatware - Juliska

Page 59
dinnerware - Lenox; flatware - Juliska

Page 60
graphically created

Page 61
lobster fork - Shreve & Co.; remainder - graphically created

Page 62
Lenox, Juliska, Nambé, Waterford, Vista Allegre, American Metalcraft, Reidel, Royal Albert, Lomonosov

Page 63
Royal Copenhagen, Lenox, Juliska, Arte Italica, Haviland, Homer Laughlin, Waterford, Bon Chef, American Metalcraft, Harold Import, Libbey, Royal Bavarian Crystal

Page 64
glassware - Reidel; wine - Far Nienthe

Page 65
glassware - Waterford, Riedel, Libbey, Godinger, Fox Run

Page 66
glassware - Libbey

Page 67
Fox Run, Waterford, Johnson Rose, Vagabond House, Rosle, OXO, NorPro, Laguiole, Metrokane, Screwpull, Opromo, OH-SO, Fran Mara, Inc., Juliska, Libbey, West Bend, Vollrath, Zodiax, Mariposa

Page 69
charger and napkin - graphically created; flatware - International Silver

Back Cover
glassware - Libbey, Reidel, Juliska, Waterford; napkin ring, dinnerware and flatware by Juliska; napkin - Kim Seybert; champagne bucket and serving platter - graphically created

Bibliography and sources

Art of the Table
    by Suzanne Von Drachenfels
New Manners for New Times
    by Letitia Baldrige
Little Book of Etiquette
    by Dorothea Johnson
President's Table
    by Barry H. Landau
Sterling Silver Flatware for Dining Elegance
    by Richard Osterberg

Handbook for Hosts: A Practical Guide to Party Planning and Gracious Entertaining
    by Adam Bluestein and Town & Country
The Rituals of Dinner
    by Margaret Visser

Recommended books
Many of the menu selections listed throughout the book can be found in these cookbooks:

Simply Zov Cookbook: Rustic Classics with a Mediterranean Twist
Zov: Recipes and Memories from the Heart
    by Zov Karamardian

Melissa's 50 Best Plants on the Planet
Melissa's Everyday Cooking with Organic Produce
Melissa's Great Book of Produce
    by Cathy Thomas
    cathythomascooks.com
    melissas.com

Other recommended books
Christmas with Dickens
    By Cedric Charles Dickens with David and Betty Dickens
    Jackprises.com

Food and Wine Cocktails 2014
    10th Anniversary Edition

Culinary School
Rosemarie attended "Le Calabash," a cooking school in Loire Valley, France with her two grandchildren in the summer of 2014. The school's motto is "let's take a walk on the wild side" — talk about a week of truly memorable cooking extravaganzas!

Learn to cook without boundaries. Consider attending their school and purchasing their new book:
Le Calabash, a Culinary Adventure
    by Alison and Sidney Bond
    lecalabash.com

Index

Thank You

We wish to thank the following individuals and businesses for their contributions to this book.

Dorothea Johnson, founder of the Protocol School of Washington, whom we admire more and more for her trailblazing work in the field of dining and etiquette

Don Kingsborough, for your advice, hand-holding, marketing expertise and getting this book off the ground and launched

Dr. K. Allen Pedersen, for your astounding generosity and integral participation in the creation of *"Which Fork Do I Use?"*

Kathy Lee, graphic artist, for your friendship, patience, creativity and guidance

Paulette Burnard, editor, for injecting humor and creative wordsmithing

Robyn Cathey, for early work with our technology and marketing strategies

Sev Spagnolie, MPS Printing, for your recommendations, generousity and for the initial kickoff of *"Which Fork Do I Use?"*

Tom Maks and the employees at Maks Wood Products, for sharing your office space and for your tolerance as the project progressed.

Draeger's at Blackhawk Plaza and Misto Lino in Danville, CA, for inspiration from your trendy merchandise

Jerry deCastro and Helen Grima, Litho Process Printing, for advice and allowing us to take over your office space

Randy Harvey, PhD, JD, for your enthusiastic support and speedy legal advice

A special thank you to our friends and family who have offered opinions, talent and experiences that have helped to make this book better. Mostly thank you for your encouragement and faith in us. If you don't see your name on this page, please know it's in our hearts.

Lisa Baer	Sondra Jameson	Lisa Pinguelo
Rosemary Baldo	Rebecca Kingsborough	Miki Sakata Pinguelo
Gianna Burns	Debra Miglia	Caitlin Scott
Thomy Clements	Lisa Molinari	Ildiko Scott
Barbara Faunce	Sandy Molinari	Lauren Scott
James Furlo	Vanessa Pass	Damien Secore
Alana Hay	Leslie Pinguelo	Deanna Swanstrom
		Caroline Taylor

~ Rosemarie and Linda

Know someone who'd enjoy "Which Fork Do I Use?"

TO ORDER:

Visit our website: mannerssimply.com

Email: orders@mannerssimply.com

Call: (925) 736-2880

Fax: (925) 406-4565

Or mail the form below to:
P. O. Box 2676, Danville, California 94526

All books are sent by USPS Standard Ground
If you want expedited service, please call (925) 736-2880

Quantity	$24.95 each	Total Price
Local Tax		
Shipping and Handling (one book)	$5.95	
GRAND TOTAL		

PAYMENT ENCLOSED:

☐ Visa

☐ MasterCard

☐ American Express

☐ Discover

☐ PayPal (please visit our web page: mannerssimply.com)

☐ Check or Money Order

ADDRESS ASSOCIATED WITH ACCOUNT:

Name on card_____

Card no._____ Exp. date_____

Street address_____

City, State, Zip Code_____

Email address_____

Phone number_____
Please fill out ALL of the above. You will receive confirmation by e-mail.

SHIPPING ADDRESS (if different from above):

First and last name_____

Street address_____

City, State, Zip Code_____